Eminent Hipsters

Eminent Hipsters

Donald
FAGEN VIKING

VIKING
Published by the Penguin Group
Penguin Group (USA) LLC
375 Hudson Street
New York, New York 10014

USA | Canada | UK | Ireland | Australia | New Zealand | India | South Africa | China
penguin.com
A Penguin Random House Company

First published by Viking Penguin, a member of Penguin Group (USA) LLC, 2013

Portions of this book appeared in different form in *Harper's Bazaar*, *Jazz Times*, *Premiere*, and *Slate*.

Grateful acknowledgment is made for permission to reprint excerpts from the following copyrighted works:

"Heebie Jeebies" by Boyd Atkins. Copyright © 1926 Universal Music Corp. Copyright renewed. All rights reserved. Used by permission. Reprinted with permission of Hal Leonard Corporation.
"Deacon Blues," words and music by Walter Becker and Donald Fagen. Copyright © 1977, 1978 Universal Music Corp. Copyright renewed. All rights reserved. Used by permission. Reprinted with permission of Hal Leonard Corporation.
"The Hip Gan" from "The Tales of Lord Buckley" by Lord Buckley. Used by permission.
"Hell Hound On My Trail," words and music by Robert Johnson. Copyright © (1978), 1990, 1991 MPCA King of Spades (SESAC) and Claud L. Johnson (SESAC). Administered by MPCA Music, LLC. All rights reserved. Reprinted with permission of Hal Leonard Corporation.
"Jumpin' with Symphony Sid," lyrics by King Pleasure, music by Lester Young. © 1953 (renewed) Unichappell Music Inc., Elvis Presley Music Inc. and EMI Unart Catalog Inc. All rights in the U.S. administered by Unichappell Music Inc. All rights reserved. "Jumpin' with Symphony Sid," words by Buddy Feyne, music by Lester Young. Copyright © 1949, 1953 (renewed 1977) Atlantic Music Corp., Travis Music Co. and EMI U Catalog Inc. International copyright secured. All rights reserved. Reprinted with permission of Hal Leonard Music.
"Plastic People" by Frank Zappa. Used by permission of Munchkin Music.

LIBRARY OF CONGRESS CATALOGING-IN-PUBLICATION DATA
Fagen, Donald.
Eminent hipsters / Donald Fagen.
pages   cm
ISBN 978-0-670-02551-0
1. Fagen, Donald, 1948– 2. Rock musicians—United States—Biography. I. Title.
ML420.F2E45 2013
781.64092—dc23
[B]
2013017054

Printed in the United States of America
10 9 8 7 6 5 4 3 2 1

Set in Palatino with Noa display | Designed by Carla Bolte

Penguin is committed to publishing works of quality and integrity. In that spirit, we are proud to offer this book to our readers; however, the story, the experiences, and the words are the author's alone.

For Libby

Contents

Introduction

You may be thinking, oh no, another rock-and-roll geezer making a last desperate bid for mainstream integrity by putting out a book of belles lettres. The fact is, until I got out of high school, I was pretty sure I'd end up in journalism or teaching English or working in a bookstore or something along those lines. I had a little piano trio in high school but, by jazz standards, I was strictly an amateur. Then it was the summer of '65 and my friend Pete gave me that psychedelic sugar cube. After the universe stopped squirming around and the colors dimmed down a bit, I was left with a new sense of possibility. When I started college that fall, I noticed that guys who played even worse than I did were all in bands and seemed to be having major fun. By the time I hooked up with my partner, Walter Becker, a couple of years later, I'd pretty much given up on a literary career.

In the mid-eighties, when I was in the midst of a severe episode of creative torpor, Susan Lyne, who was starting up *Premiere* magazine, asked if I'd be interested in writing a film music column. Although I didn't know that much about the subject, I'd seen a lot of movies and I thought it might be therapeutic. It turned out it was, and Susan didn't seem to mind if the stuff I turned in was a little on the self-indulgent side. I got a lot of nice mail and kept writing.

From time to time, people have suggested that the pieces I've written over the last thirty years might be arrayed in such a way as to form a kind of art-o-biography—that is, how the stuff I read and heard when I was growing up affected (stretched, skewed, mangled) my little brain. That's the organizing principle here. When my editor, Paul Slovak, agreed that my grouchy tour journal from the summer of 2012 might be entertaining, we stuffed that in too. Also written especially for this book: an account of my college days and an essay on the magnificent Boswell Sisters. I don't want to be a critic. It's fun only if I'm writing about creative work that, as Willie "The Lion" Smith would say, is "what you call . . . *real good.*"

You'll find that many chapters in this book are about people and things that intersected with my life when I was a kid. I apologize up front: I tried to grow up. Honest. Didn't quite happen. I guess I'm someone for whom youth still seems more real than the present, or the half century in between. And why not? I'm deeply underwhelmed by most contemporary art, literature, music, films, TV, the heinous little phones, money talk, real estate talk, all that stuff. The Internet, which at first seemed so fascinating, appears to be evolving into something even worse than TV, but we'll see.

So here it is. Folks around my age might recognize incidental references to various Cold War and "counterculture" phenomena: Oldsmobiles, fish sticks, nuclear war, Bosco, psychedelic drugs, Haight-Ashbury, the "Groovy" murders. My mom, my dad and my baby sister Susan make occasional cameos. But the main subjects are the talented musicians, writers and performers from a universe beyond suburban New Jersey who showed me how to interpret my own world. There are count-less definitions of the word "hipster." In the title of this book, I'm using it to refer to artists whose origins lie outside the main-stream or who creatively exploit material from the margin or who, merely because they live in a freaky space, have enough distance to see some truth.

One more thing: some folks bug out when they see their names in print. On the advice of the Penguin legal department—I know, that sounds so cute—I've changed the names of a few people and places.

DF, January 2013

Eminent Hipsters

Boswells' Version

The first jazz I remember hearing was in my cousin Barbara's base-ment. Barbara was a knockout, gorgeous and curvy, a great dancer, and hip too. Hanging out at jazz clubs in the Village, she had no trouble get-ting to know the major players, including Miles and Monk. (For a while she was married to Phil Woods's piano player Mike Melillo.) On family visits, she'd bring her little cousins down to the basement, where she'd play us LPs by the hard boppers—Wynton Kelly, Hank Mobley, Johnny Griffin and others. But it was my mom who introduced me to the music of the great Connie Boswell and her sisters.

For what it's worth, my mother's married name, Elinor Fagen, was just a couple of letters away from Billie Holiday's given name: Eleanora Fagan. Although no Lady Day, my mother was a fine swing singer who from the age of five through her teen years worked with a trio in a hotel in the Catskills—the "Jewish Alps." Her career as "Ellen Ross" came to an end at sixteen when stage fright prevented her from walking up to the micro-phone on *Major Bowes Amateur Hour*, a radio program that was the *American Idol* of its time. After that, she performed only at ladies' club functions and while she was at her housewifely chores, waking the kids up, vacuuming, cooking and cleaning.

Ellie had very specific taste in popular singers. She was a

connoisseur of what jazz people refer to as "phrasing," the way notes or groups of notes are precisely placed, syncopated or "swung," as they used to say in the thirties. Some of her favorites were Billie, Peggy Lee, Helen Humes, Frances Faye, Ethel Waters, Anita O'Day and the now forgotten Gertrude Niesen. She loved Judy Garland and, of course, the bobby-soxer's main man, Frank Sinatra ("I hate him, but I love him!"). She thought that Fred Astaire was underappreciated as a singer, and often mentioned Cliff Edwards, who, as "Ukulele Ike," was a big star in the twenties and thirties. Edwards had a late career bump in the fifties as the voice of Disney's Jiminy Cricket.

Once, in an old musical we were watching on *Million Dollar Movie*, a pretty, healthy-looking young woman sat on a bench in a nightclub and sang a number. My mother said, "Do you know who that is? That's Connie Boswell. She was crippled from polio, but she was the best." Years later, when I became familiar with the early work of Connie and her two sisters, I discovered that the Boswells had created a body of work rivaling that of Duke Ellington.

The Boswell Sisters—Martha, Connie and Helvetia (called Vet)—grew up during the 1920s in a big white house in New Orleans, on Camp Street, near the Garden District. The cause of Connie's disability was either polio or, as she used to tell it, a nasty soapbox-on-wheels accident. In any case, after the age of four, she could walk only a few steps at a time. Their father, Alfred, a well-to-do executive and amateur musician with Italian roots, sent his daughters to study music with a local professor. All three showed great talent, and they started performing chamber music at local venues at an early age—Martha on piano, Connie on cello, Vet on violin. But this was New Orleans in the Jazz Age, and the girls couldn't escape the syncopated music they heard all around them every day. They listened to the sounds coming from black bars and churches, and attended shows at the local "chitlin' circuit" theater (whites were allowed to sit in the balcony for the Saturday "Midnight Frolic"). They bought hot jazz records by Bix Beiderbecke and the Wolverines, and blues sides by the Smiths (Mamie and Bessie). As Martha told an interviewer in 1925:

> We studied classical music, compositions by the world's artist(s) for more than seven years and were being prepared for the stage and a concert tour throughout the United States, but the saxophone got us . . .

By the mid-twenties, the girls had started playing the new music and focusing on the sound of their distinctive three-part vocal harmony. Vet switched to banjo and Connie was playing a raucous tenor sax. Young jazz players, especially the Italian-American contingent, started hanging out in the Boswells' parlor. There were Louis Prima and his brother Leon, Tony Parenti and Leon Roppolo, and the legendary cornetist Emmett Hardy (said to be Bix's mentor), who quickly became enamored of the beautiful Martha (he died of tuberculosis, at twenty-three). The boys must have been astonished to find three white, upper-middle-class girls so deeply immersed in the rhythms of the city.

On "Cryin' Blues," one of two sides recorded in 1925 by a Victor talent scout, Connie, then eighteen, is already a convincing blues shouter in the Mamie Smith mode. Earlier, there had been white blues singers in minstrelsy and vaudeville, but, unlike Mae West or Sophie Tucker (Tucker actually hired Mamie Smith to give her blues lessons), Connie sings with an authentic rhythmic feel and her bent notes are Bourbon Street perfect. Moreover, because her Big Easy accent matches up with the blues inflections, the listener never experiences any of that "This ain't right" ethnic or class tension that can vitiate the performance of an otherwise talented blues singer.

In 1929, after enduring a grungy cross-country vaudeville tour, the Sisters landed in Hollywood, where, a year later, they waxed some sides for the Okeh label. With "Heebie Jeebies," we can hear the Boswells beginning to apply their classical background to some hot material. "Heebie Jeebies," written by New Orleans altoist Boyd Atkins, had been made famous by Louis Armstrong and His Hot Five in a 1926 recording that included a famous scat chorus. Actually, the original record is nothing much, just a hokum (novelty) number that gives Armstrong a chance to do his thing. The Boswells could have just remade the record in their key. Instead, they bust the piece out by giving it a nuanced dramatic structure complete with tempo changes, ritenutos (slowdowns), additional lyrics, new melodic material, special vocal effects and their unmatchable group dynamics. This process would become the Boswells' signature.

After a wordless introduction, the Sisters rip into the chorus. They've got the heebie jeebie blues and the only cure is to bring the feeling to critical mass by doing the heebie jeebie dance. Then Martha's piano slows to an easy blues tempo and Connie, in an ethereal solo, explains the situation:

I been havin' 'em—havin' 'em all day long
I got the heebies but I can't go wrong
'Cause when I got 'em I just roll along
Now listen everybody while I sing this song . . .

The newly composed melody and lyrics in this section totally change the character of the piece. Suddenly, having a case of the heebie jeebies isn't all that funny. It's a specific sort of agitated depression, and moreover, now stated by Connie as a gentle blues, it's a state of mind specific to women. Banishing the blue devils with a beat, Martha and Vet then join in at the faster tempo. One chorus later, they paraphrase Armstrong's scat vocal, but arranged as an ensemble for all three voices. Finally, they correct the Hot Fives' famously flubbed hokum finish, and all is well again on Camp Street. The Boswells have transformed Armstrong's party tune into a sonic moving picture of a woman's inner life over a day's time. And all this without sacrificing any jazz heat.

By 1931, the Boswells had caught on, especially with young fans, and they had begun to work with Jack Kapp at Brunswick Records in New York. In the studio, Kapp brought the girls together with the best musicians in the city (i.e., the best white musicians). The core group, mostly out of the Dorsey Brothers' nascent band, included Jimmy and Tommy Dorsey on alto sax and trombone, guitarist Eddie Lang and his partner Joe Venuti on violin, trumpeters Jack Purvis, Manny Klein and Bunny Berigan, pianist Artie Schutt, bassist Joe Tarto, and drummers Stan King and Chauncey Morehouse.

As Joe Tarto testified, the collaboration of the Boswells and the band was "a whole new idea of voices and instruments together." Years later, Connie described the process to interviewer Michael Brooks:

> Most of our Brunswick sessions were cut between midnight and dawn. We'd finish up our show at the Paramount or the Roxy, then go over to Plunkett's, a tiny bar on Fifty-third Street about four doors off Broadway frequented by New York studio, pit and dance band musicians and get the Dorseys, Bunny Berigan, Manny Klein, Stan King and the rest of the boys. Then there'd be a sobering-up session while we pumped black coffee into them and we'd finally get to recording. In those days we didn't have tape but recorded directly onto wax. The boys'd often be juiced and there'd be mistakes galore. Sometimes we'd spoil twenty to thirty waxes before we'd get an acceptable take. That would be labeled Take "A" and we'd ruin a few more and get to Take "B" and then so on. I used to write the arrangements and they were pretty tightly scored although I always tried to get a loose, swinging sound and give the boys room to blow. They were just the greatest bunch of fellas to work with: crazy, but all wonderful musicians who understood exactly what we were trying to do and we had a ball, I can tell ya.

In other interviews, Connie gives Martha and Vet more credit for their creative input. The unworldly precision of the group singing alone proves that some sort of sibling telepathy was in operation. Said Vet:

I'd be in the bedroom, Martha would be in the kitchen and Connie in the living room, and we'd start singing the same song at the same time and in the same key. That's how in tune we were to each other.

To keep things running smoothly, the Dorseys' arranger, young Glenn Miller, was on hand to quickly write out ideas for the players as they came up.

Harry Woods's tune "We Just Couldn't Say Good-bye" was a popular one in 1932, spawning versions by Guy Lombardo and Mildred Bailey as well as the Boswells. It's interesting to compare the Sisters' version with one recorded just ten days later by Annette Hanshaw at a session including some of the same players. Hanshaw, promoted as "The Personality Girl," relied more on her flapperesque charm than any excess of musical talent, but she had a kind of loosey-goosey style that seemed to work, especially when teamed with fine players like Lang and Venuti.

After the introduction, Hanshaw sings the tune in her usual fashion, sounding both nervous and slightly tipsy. Benny Goodman comes to the rescue with some flashy support on clarinet. Soon, Joe Venuti's violin enters, doubling the melody. A pause for a trumpet line by Phil Napoleon, and then there's a nice moment when everything slows down and Hanshaw, accompanied only by Rube Bloom's piano, sings the verse of the song, which has been transported from its usual position at the top. When the refrain comes back in tempo, Hanshaw scats and ad-libs, trading off with the soloists. Then there's a bit of hokum. After the lines,

The chair and then the sofa broke right down and cried
I'll tell you confidentially the tears were hard to hide

the trumpet and clarinet "act" them out instrumentally. There's even a ticking clock sound effect accompanying a line about the clock striking twelve. For me, the whimsy in the lyric satisfies without these goofy asides: the mood has been broken. Even so, it's a cute effort, and the level of musicianship raises it above the standard market value of the time.

The Boswells' rendition starts out at a slower tempo, with Bunny Berigan immediately establishing a down-home New Orleans feel. Sounding a bit like Ethel Waters, Connie sings the tune down once, her intonation, as always, dead-on. Whenever she comes to the hook line, "We couldn't say good-bye," she reaches up an octave and, thrillingly, blue-notes (flats) the third. Prefiguring the Hanshaw recording, the verse has also been moved forward. But instead of the normal tempo drop, the band speeds up and the girls sing the verse in harmony. And for giggles, they've tossed the original chord progression and substituted a modernistic sequence of chords that changes the key from F major to F minor. The juxtaposition is startling: it's as if we've been instantly teleported from the sleepy Delta to Times Square on Saturday night.

In order to accommodate a chromatic melody line in the last bar, they've also rewritten some of the lyrics. As this manic, urban mood continues into the main body of the song, a chord pattern is set up that changes the key center from F major to D major every other bar. It's the kind of Gershwin-like effect that Otis Redding and Steve Cropper would employ at Stax sessions some thirty years later. Connie takes the bridge alone and then the girls come back in for the last shout chorus, with Connie adding some wailing licks at the finish for good measure. The Boswells have taken care that, from the downbeat to the last cymbal hit, there's not a boring bar in this arrangement.

Among the seventy-five or so tracks that the Boswells recorded from 1931 to 1936, it's hard to find one in which they didn't use their subversive genius to enrich the given raw material. Aside from the innovations already mentioned, they imitated jazz instrumental effects with their voices, devised tricky phrasing, switched from straight time to swing time, employed "speed singing" and even raced through whole choruses in "Boswellese," a childhood language of their own invention ("love" would break down to, I think, "luggle-duv"). They may not have invented the word "yowzah," but, as far as I've been able to find, the first recorded "yowzah" occurs on their 1932 version of "The Sentimental Gentleman from Georgia."

When singing solo passages, Connie—this formidable musician in a Louisiana belle's ball gown—is simultaneously hot and cool: she's emotionally connected to the lyric and at the same time reveals a self-reflexive, ironic quality that's astonishing for the era. Her self-awareness as an artist (if not her sense of modesty) is borne out by quotes from interviews in later years:

> At that time I'm sure that to the average ear we must have sounded like little green people from outer space . . . We revolutionized not only the style of singing, the beat, the placing of voices, the way-out harmony, but also the musical world in

general . . . I used to work wee hours in the morning, but Martha and Vet were loaded with talent and contributed much to the trio arrangements. The band background, intros, fill-ins, and special endings were usually planned by me. Some parts were as free as the breeze, while others were kept right in the saddle . . .

If you listen you will hear that Jimmy Dorsey, Tommy Dorsey, Bunny Berigan, all those fellas, though they were great individually, they played as a group completely different . . . When they played for us, we sang and we gave them certain little breaks and things we wanted them to do back of us that made them sound completely different on our records than they did on anybody else's.

Jack Kapp, always apprehensive about the commercial potential of the Sisters' work, often clashed with Connie about the eccentric treatment of the material. After he moved the group to his new label, American Decca, in 1935, he was able to exert more control, especially over the tracks Connie recorded as a solo artist. Her vocals, while never less than lovely, started to lose their drive and the arrangements became more conventional. A year later, Martha and Vet retired to tend to their new husbands and families, leaving Connie, who had married their manager, to continue on her own. Although Connie's career bubbled along nicely up through the war years, she was never to be quite the innovator she was when she sang with her sisters. After the breakup, the Boswell-worshipping Andrews Sisters, employing a more accessible version of their basic harmony style, stepped into the vacuum and went on to great commercial glory. But the Jazz Age was over. The great swing bands (with a few exceptions) collapsed and the era of the celebrity soloist had begun.

Connie, now Connee (don't ask), obliged to share the stage with entertainers like Bing Crosby and Judy Garland and Doris Day—folks who could walk and dance and strut in front of movie cameras—couldn't compete. When she performed with her sisters, Connie had usually been seated next to Martha on the piano bench with Vet standing close behind: three belles in the parlor made a nice picture. Alone, Connie struggled to make up for her disability with cybernetic help: special chairs or braces with wheels worn under her flowing skirts. But by the late forties, her star had grown dimmer. It was fine for Louis Armstrong to stand under the lights sweating bullets and waving that handkerchief around, but a white woman, no matter how good she sounded, needed to be standing up behind the mic, projecting confidence, looking good.

After the invention of the long-playing disc reinvigorated the record business in the fifties, Connie had a last hurrah with a few well-produced jazz and pop LPs. Her final recording, in 1962, was a rockabilly tune she wrote herself: "You Ain't Got Nothin'." Her range had dropped, but Connie was more than comfortable singing over the boogie bass and twanging guitar, sounding a bit like a toned-down Wanda Jackson or Brenda Lee. At fifty-five, more so than any of her contemporaries, she was still a rhythm gal through and through.

One wonders what trajectory Connie's life might have followed if not for the complex challenges presented by her disability. On the other hand, the connection between Connie's childhood misfortunes and her early work might stand in support of Edmund Wilson's theory of "the wound and the bow." Wilson suggests that the themes of an artist's work represent a healing reenactment of some primal injury—in this case, a literal, physical injury. Confronted with a piece of material—a popular song—Connie's instinct was to pull it apart, reorganize its parts and reshape it into something richer than the original. Like the painter Frida Kahlo, born in the same year, Connie was able to exploit her physical calamity in the formation of her art using similar means: irony, startling juxtaposition of events, even surrealism. Fortunately for Connie, she was able to rely on Martha and Vet, who, from childhood, were enlisted as both her caretakers and her willing conspirators.

Of course, the first time you hear these dynamic sides from the beginning of the last century, none of this is immediately apparent. Whatever suffering might have contributed to the Boswells' artistry has been transformed by some alchemy of the human spirit into pure joy. From the downbeat, we're transported to Jazz Age New Orleans: we hear the music that was in the streets, in the churches, in the improvisations of the piano professors of Storyville, and the laughter of three teenage girls for whom, in the words of W. S. Gilbert's three little maids from school, "life is a joke that's just begun."

Henry Mancini's
Anomie Deluxe

In the late fifties and early sixties, Henry Mancini's music was omnipresent: on TV, in films and featured in select elevators all over the world. For many, his music, along with that of the popular Dave Brubeck Quartet, served as an introduction to the sound of modern jazz.

I must have been about eight years old when my father, like so many other second-generation American dads, decided to get his family the hell out of the city and make a run at upward mobility in the suburbs. After a couple of years and a few false starts, we finally settled into a ranch-style home nestled among hundreds of its near-identical brothers in Kendall Park, New Jersey, a typical housing development circa 1957. The development was not very developed. I was not happy.

Sawdust still hung in the air. To walk out of the sliding glass doors onto the slab of concrete that was the patio and stare across an ocean of mud at one's doppelganger neighbors was, well, awesome. My parents, gazing out the window of the kitchen of the future, delighted in the open space, the gently curving streets and the streamlined look of the cream Olds Dynamic 88 all cozy in its carport. But for me, a subterranean in gestation with a real nasty case of otherness, it was a prison. I'd been framed and sentenced to a long stretch at hard labor in Squaresville.

The days were filled with whatever a fifth grader's days are filled with. In the evening, after wolfing down a few servings of fish sticks, I'd fling myself onto the couch in the family room. My dad would sit at the card table doing take-home work on his yellow accounting pad. My mother would be in the kitchen eliminating microscopic particles of food from the counters. My baby sister, Susan, would be flinging wads of Play-Doh at the wall. Of course, the TV would be on. Monday nights at nine, we watched *Peter Gunn*.

Beatsters! Brothers in the subculture of the Early Resigned! Reminisce with me: after a suspenseful, highly stylized teaser, we'd thrill to the driving boogie ostinato on bass, doubled in the lowest octaves of the piano and tripled by a raunchy surf guitar, the same bar repeated throughout, never changing. The drummer's on auto-cook. Close-voiced brass plays the angular, blues-based theme. On the screen we see the title animation, a bogus abstract expressionist canvas with cryptic, splattery forms pulsing in the foreground. Even then we may have known it was jive, but who cared? The titles, action-painted on top of all this, told us the show was created by Blake Edwards and that the music was by Henry Mancini.

During the fifties there had been a number of TV shows that exploited the combination of film noir and jazz-based music, such as *Naked City* and *Richard Diamond* and *M Squad*. But 1958's *Peter Gunn* was the noirest of them all. Edwards's update of the Chandleresque detective story, with its tense visual style, demanded a suitably chilled-out sound track, and Mancini, who had scored Orson Welles's *Touch of Evil* that same year, seemed to understand what this show was all about: style, and nothing much else in particular. "The *Miami Vice* of its time," a friend of mine remarked. Craig Stevens as Gunn would cruise around a narcotized and vulgarly luxurious Los Angeles like Cary Grant on Miltown, doing his job of detection and occasionally alighting at Mother's, a nightclub where his main squeeze, Edie, worked as a jazz singer. (The slow make-out scenes between Gunn and Edie, played by Lola Albright, seemed not to belong in the family room, and it was no cinch trying to conceal my erotic dithers from my parents.) Every so often, he'd check in with his pal Lieutenant Jacoby, the good cop. But Gunn may as well have been drifting through a landscape of boomerangs and parallelograms, so little did the plots matter. What counted was the sense that these people had been around the block a few times, had found a way to live amid the stultifying sleaziness of the modern world, keeping their emotions under control except for occasional spasms of sex and violence.

Of course, these weren't authentic hipsters, Mailer's White Negroes or Kerouac's Beats. Gunn, Edie and Jacoby were supposed to be more like pallies of Sinatra or James Bond, streetwise swingers: they were hip, but they could operate in the straight world with an existential efficiency. And yet, so strong was the pull toward an alternate way of life that, at least to a hyperaesthetic ten-year-old, the show's whole gestalt made sense. It spoke to my condition. I could identify with Gunn's outsider stance and admire his improvised lifestyle without venturing outside the perimeter of comfort and convenience my parents had provided. To the contrary, Edwards's camera eye seemed to take a carnal interest in the luxe and leisure objects of the period, focusing on Scandinavian furniture, potted palms, light wood paneling and sleek shark-finned convertibles. It was, in fact, all the same stuff my parents adored, but darkened with a tablespoon of alienation and danger. Sort of like seeing a smiling Pan Am pilot climb out of his 707 with a copy of *La Nausée* sticking out of his back pocket.

Mancini didn't have to look far to find the appropriate sound to enhance Edwards's vision of anomie deluxe. At the time, West Coast jazz (essentially, white bop) was being offered to college kids as part of the same package that included the Beats, open-toed sandals and psychoanalysis. The white bopper playing a subdued parlor jazz was an easier sell than his black counterpart. Sure, the image spoke, the crew-cut cool-schoolers may be, like the black boppers, wigged out, self-destructive hopheads (something you, the middle class, are fascinated by), but they're also safely Caucasian and get to spend a lot of time at Hermosa Beach.

Nevertheless, there were a lot of very talented players on the coast and Mancini was canny enough to bring them into the studio to record the *Gunn* scores. Future film score titan John Williams was the piano player. The studio band also included trumpeter Pete Candoli, brothers Ted and Dick Nash (reeds and trombone), guitarist Bob Bain, drummer Jack Sperling and vibraphonist Larry Bunker. The idiom he used was largely out of Gil Evans and other progressive arrangers plus the odd shot of rhythm and blues. He utilized the unconventional, spare instrumentation associated with the cool school: French horns, vibraphone, electric guitar and—Mancini's specialty—a very active flute section, including both alto flute and the rarely used bass flute. Instruments were often individually miked to bring out the detail. For small groups, Mancini hijacked the elegant "locked hands" voicing style associated with pianists Milt Buckner and George Shearing. There was a lot of empty space. It was real cool.

Mancini's albums of music from the *Peter Gunn* series and the spin-off show, *Mr. Lucky*, sold in the zillions, and I was one of the proud consumers. The tunes had titles like "Dreamsville" and "A Profound Gass." The music inspired me to learn more about jazz and the extramusical artifacts of the jazz life. I listened to late-night jazz jocks broadcasting out of Manhattan and got a subscription to *Down Beat*, which had lots of live-action photos of the top players. I tried to get through a few Kerouac novels.

Out of these fragments of hip and hype I constructed in my mind a kind of Disneyland of Cool. I could imagine musicians cruising up and down Central Avenue in cartoon Studebakers and finally assembling in a large sound studio. Folding chairs, music stands. The cats are sitting in a semicircle around a couple of those enormous RCA microphones on boom stands, some in two-tone shirts with roll collars, others in Hawaiian gear and bop glasses. Horns are slipped out of canvas gig bags. There's a potted palm in the corner. Hank Mancini walks in, not the tanned, carefully coiffed entertainer of later years, but the introspective young professional as pictured on his late-fifties album covers. Everybody's smoking Pall Malls or some other powerful nonfilter cigarettes. Hank hands out the parts. When they run down the chart, a thick membrane of sound flows forth and hovers in the room. It sounds incredibly plush. Behind the glass, the engineers at the console are digging it. Maybe a few smokin' chicks in black tights fall by. And so on.

The next time I saw Henry Mancini's name was in the credit roll of *Breakfast at Tiffany's*, also directed by our man Blake Edwards. I was thirteen and ready for love. When the venal waif Holly Golightly (Audrey Hepburn) got out of that cab on Fifth Avenue in a black dress and pearls in the early morning, I wanted to sip her through a straw.

Whenever I mention this picture to someone around my age, a strange, tragic smile flits across his or her face as if in remembrance of an old lover. Even those who dismiss the film as a piece of typical Hollywood fluff that took the sting out of Capote's original story, blah, blah, are betrayed by a wetness in the eyes, a heaving chest and an occasional shudder of bliss/pain. Obviously, some part of the nervous system wants to acknowledge the film's impact.

Edwards's special interest in marginality in an expensive setting made him a good choice for this urban romance, but it was his huckleberry friend Hank who really came through. We may have OD'd on "Moon River" long ago, but, as played on the harmonica during that opening scene, it still does the job. The harmonica, an instrument associated with children, stands in for Holly's rural origins (innocence) and contrasts with the rich orchestration and what you're seeing on the screen (Tiffany's, Givenchy shades, sophistication). It's a great effect, much imitated since. Later on, Hepburn sits on the fire escape and sings "Moon River" while accompanying herself on the guitar. She's wearing pedal pushers and a sweatshirt. In Capote's novel, she sings, more appropriately, a mournful country ballad, but why quibble with perfection?

As in *Peter Gunn*, the city is presented as a grid of luxe through which the outsider characters, Holly and Paul, drift. To score the scenes in which they goof around town, Mancini used a mixed chorus singing in a skidoo-be-doo scat style similar to that of the Modernaires or the Mel-Tones. This was a little twee for my taste. By 1961 I was starting to wise up about jazz, and I felt that Hank, by exploiting this blanched-out idiom from the previous decade, had exposed himself as a bit of a moldy fig. Nevertheless, it enhanced the concept of a carefree, womblike Manhattan in which the bohemian ruled with a magical, child-like omnipotence. In high school I would have given anything to preserve that sanctified state, to rescue Holly from herself (from growing up, being corrupted), to goof around an enchanted Manhattan with some wild thing forever, scat singers always on call to back us up.

Eventually, my quest for relevance and authenticity (plus a not unsound instinct as to where the most desirable girls were gathering) propelled me into a phase where even the greatest jazz—Ellington, Miles, Mingus, Monk—seemed slick and sexually coy, and I turned to blues and soul music and Bob Dylan. I started reading about pop art and Timothy Leary's experiments at Harvard. I went to a lot of Brit movies of the kitchen-sink school. The language of hip was changing.

In his own way Blake Edwards was sensitive to this shift in

consciousness. Super-suave Peter Gunn had evolved into Inspector Clouseau, who tries to stay cool but finds the world just too opposed to the notion. The luxe is still there but the alienation is played for laughs. The expensive objects (custom pool cues, cigarette lighters, etc.) literally attack Clouseau. When Edwards began to sabotage his own hero, it should have been a tip-off as to what was coming. Egos were cracking. Self-image and sexual identity got hazy around the edges. When Clouseau runs across a cool jazz combo in *A Shot in the Dark*, they're gigging in a nudist colony and they're in their birthday suits. The old, heavily defended hipster has literally been stripped naked. As for the music in the Pink Panther films, it has become an extravagant parody of coolness—it's funny because it's too spooky, too cool to be believed.

By the time I left suburbia to go off to college in 1965, Mancini seemed a quaint enthusiasm. If I thought about him at all, he would have seemed, at best, a popularizer of jazz, a dependable Hollywood professional. I'm sure some guys in my dorm would have seen him as an insidious agent of the "culture industry" that was devouring America's native art form and packaging it for mass consumption. Although I didn't think in those terms, by the late sixties Hank had metamorphosed, certainly in my mind, into an incredible square. His popular tunes from films, his recordings and pops concert appearances had turned him into a Grammy-laden institution of American entertainment. The concept of hip had exploded into the culture in a new form, and Mancini (and mainstream jazz in general) was definitely not part of it, despite all those boogaloo beats that started creeping into his scores. For a while, Mancini and the younger contender Burt Bacharach (who arguably was to soul music what Mancini was to jazz) seemed to be engaged in a series of bossa nova wars (Bacharach won at least one round with the Manciniesque "The Look of Love," sung by Dusty Springfield in the Peter Sellers film *Casino Royale*). Occasionally I'd see a photo of Mancini in those days, looking amiably affluent in a Hatari bush jacket with epaulets, fashionably long sideburns, a Rodeo Drive smile and a very expensive watch: a pleasant, cheerful-looking California person. Somewhere in there he had a TV show, *The Mancini Generation*. Yow.

In the irony-saturated eighties, though, New Wavers and punk bands from a generation even more tube-irradiated than mine transmuted the *Peter Gunn* theme into a kind of No Wave national anthem. Bands like the Lounge Lizards played "fake jazz" on purpose and, even now, the downtown art-rock crowd still can't seem to get enough of Hank. There's an orchestra in Paraguay that plays his stuff on instruments made from garbage.

Lately I'll be sitting at the piano and find myself picking out one of those tunes from *Peter Gunn*, one of the sweet boppy numbers, or "Days of Wine and Roses" (great changes), or even "Moon River." And I'll start thinking about a late summer sun setting over fifteen hundred identical rooftops and my family and bop glasses and Holly Golightly, about being lonesome out there in America and how that swank music connected up with so many things. Maybe I ought to get my bongos out of the attic. And in case I've given you the impression that Mancini isn't a totally happening dude, I offer you a maxim from his excellent textbook on arranging and orchestration, *Sounds and*

Scores, concerning the professional's obligation to avoid falling behind the times, musically speaking:

The milk of the sacred cows has a way of turning sour.

Not yours, my man. The sides you carved were strictly, like, young.

The Cortico-Thalamic Pause:
Growing Up Sci-Fi

It was all on the tube: Khrushchev's shoe, the Cuban Missile Crisis, Sputnik, all that stuff. One Sunday night in 1956, the Ed Sullivan Show *featured an animation called* A Short Vision *by British film-makers Peter and Joan Foldes. The film showed the effects of a hydrogen bomb explosion on humans and animals, complete with graphic renderings of the melting faces of men, women, an owl, a deer . . . Broadcast without warning on a family show that usually featured acrobats, puppets, comics and musical acts like Kate Smith and Jimmy Durante, it scared the living shit out of every kid in the country. When I arrived at school the next day, girls were still crying and teachers were grim faced. Of course, the tough kids (the soon-to-be "hoods" and "hitters") thought the whole thing was hilarious. I suppose the beatings they got from their alcoholic fathers had immunized them against easy sentiment.*

Sometime later, I started reading science fiction magazines. Many of the stories had post–World War III themes. By age fourteen, I had entered a phase where I fancied myself a sort of proto–Mad Max. I equipped myself with one of those GI utility belts, a canteen and a bowie knife, everything I needed to survive on a postapocalyptic Terra. It was every man for himself, bwah.

Man is something to be surpassed.

—*Nietzsche*

1

I was twelve, and the Science Fiction Book Club had just
sent me my first monthly selection, Anthony Boucher's two-
volume anthology, *A Treasury of Great Science Fiction*. There
was this one story by Philip K. Dick called "The Father-Thing":
An eight-year-old boy, Charles, knows that the sullen, soulless
thing that looks like his father isn't really his father. It so happens that the bogus dad, having just emerged from an egg
deposited in the garage by a buglike alien, has eaten out his
real father's insides and taken his place. Charles tries to warn
his mother, but of course she doesn't believe him. With the
help of two neighborhood pals, Charles destroys the extrater-
restrial bug, the Father-Thing and a couple more eggs containing the partially developed simulacra of Charles and his
mother. The kids have saved the world from an alien takeover.
A 1956 film based on a Jack Finney novel, *Invasion of the Body
Snatchers*—the one featuring Kevin McCarthy and a town
invaded by pod people—was another take on the same scary
idea.

Contrary to all the popular depictions of the fifties as a
time when teens danced on the counters of a thousand pastel-
dappled soda shops to the sounds of twangy guitars, the decade
was, in fact, characterized by a nail-biting paranoia. The Father-
Thing and Finney's Body Snatchers played off the fear of dis-
covering a Commie trained in the art of mind control behind
every hedge. In a way, the suspicion that one's neighbor might

be one of those nefarious Reds was even more disturbing than the threat of thermonuclear war.

The Father-Thing, though, affected me on a much more personal level. My father had just moved the family from North Jersey to the housing development on the Central Jersey flats. As we drove to the new house on the day of the move, I had tried (as I'd tried many times before) to dissuade my parents from making this terrible mistake. This time I played all my cards, reminding them that we were cutting ourselves off from our extended family back in Bergen County, from my uncles, aunts and cousins; that a change of schools would irreversibly disrupt my academic trajectory; and that the place they'd chosen to live, this "Kendall Park," was an accursed wasteland that would suck the life out of our heretofore vital family and transform it into a cryptful of mindless zombies, and so on. Sadly, my appeal fell on deaf ears.

At this point, I should probably disclose that, in truth, both my parents, though not without their eccentricities, were basically a couple of sweethearts. My dad, like a lot of Depression-bred ex-GIs, was simply looking to plunk his family down on a clean, safe green patch that was within his means. Nevertheless, at the time their rotten little bookworm of a son saw the move as a grand betrayal. In fact, I began to imagine that this was only the latest in a series of metamorphoses that was gradually transforming my parents into . . . *Parent-Things*.

In an old bleached-out color photo from the late thirties, my mother is standing in the sun in a cotton dress, laughing, her curly, reddish brown hair worn long in the style of the era.

Though her days as an entertainer were over, her professional past was still detectable in her good looks and the way she carried herself. But by the mid-fifties, a combination of forces began to effect a curious mutation.

The advent of aerosol hairspray (and the accompanying hairstyles) turned my mother's once silky locks into a rigid, lacquered hive. Around the same time, her flowing cotton print dresses began to be replaced by brightly colored jackets and pants that were apparently made of the same polymeric stuff as the beige carpet that covered almost the entire floor of our house. Despite my protests, I, too, was obliged to deck myself out in a pair of macromolecular "slacks" (beige, natch) for special occasions. Beige was the default color of the decade. The coolest girl in my high school used to throw herself down on her mom's Sahara-colored wall-to-wall carpet and crawl from one side of the living room to the other croaking, "Water . . . Water!"

As a housewife, my mother was the ideal target of the not-so-hidden persuaders of Madison Avenue, and she enthusiastically bought the whole Cold War package. The house always reeked of lemon Pledge. My sister and I drank huge glasses of milk laced with Bosco, except for a couple of exciting months when we switched to those conspicuously toxic "Flav-r Straws." My mother's cooking schedule really lightened up when she realized she could feed us Swanson's TV dinners (with apple cobbler) and the limp fish sticks of Mrs. Paul. Dessert, anyone? She bought Twinkies and Yodels by the boxload.

More disturbing was my parents' eagerness to assimilate, to blend in with mainstream American society. After all, as second- and third-generation American Jews, they were already most of the way there—they didn't even look particularly Jewish. On the other hand, I sure did, and my father, unconsciously at least, was determined to deal with it. When he was a kid, his father's paint store had been burned to the ground by home-grown Nazis, and this, combined with the trauma of his war-time experiences, left him with a complicated attitude toward his Jewish identity. It's not that he wanted to hide me in the cellar or anything. But in order to, you know, dial it down a little, he was determined to militarize my appearance until I looked like Flat-Top Joey, our newspaper boy and my father's template for cheerful, obedient, hardworking youth. So, every two weeks or so, in a ritual of supreme humiliation, he'd march me down to the barbershop for a severe crew cut. No matter: no one was ever going to mistake me for Neil Armstrong.

My primary doors of escape back then were the piano, contemporary jazz and building plastic models of fighter jets. But, mainly, I read books: the encyclopedia, novels, biography, history and especially sci-fi. In a used-book store in nearby Princeton, I soon found an antidote to "The Father-Thing" in a novel called *The World of Null-A* by A. E. van Vogt (a lot of sci-fi authors seemed to have exotic, musty-sounding names with a lot of initials). One of the strangest pulp creations of all time, it had first appeared as a serial in *Astounding Science Fiction* in 1945 and was published as a hardcover novel in 1948.

Apparently, van Vogt used to wake himself up every ninety minutes so he could write down his dreams. He'd then work the dreams into a narrative until he'd achieved what he liked to call "pulp music." Maybe that's why *The World of Null-A* reads like a combination of Raymond Chandler, *Through the Looking-Glass* and *Duck Soup*.

In the year 2560, Gilbert Gosseyn arrives in the City of the Machine to join in the annual competition to determine who tests highest in the skills of General Semantics, a Null-A (non-Aristotelian) discipline that's been adopted as the philosophical foundation of Earth society. The highest scorers get to go to Venus, where an experimental, all-Null-A society has been established. But before Gosseyn gets a chance to show his skills, he's beset by a series of mind-blowing calamities. In the first few pages of the novel, an official lie-detection device informs Gosseyn that he's not who he thinks he is: he's not from a small town in Florida; his wife is not dead, as he believed; in fact, he was never even married. Those are just memories implanted in his brain by an unknown "cosmic chess player."

A confirmed fraud, Gosseyn is thrown out of his hotel. He meets a girl who turns out to be the woman he thought was his dead wife. He's kidnapped by a gang of conspirators and accused of being an agent of the "Galactic League." They hook him up to a machine that analyzes his nervous system and then throw him into a dungeon. During an escape attempt, he's cut to pieces by machine-gun fire and, for good measure, fried by an energy beam.

When he wakes up, he's in a Venusian forest, in a spanking-new body, a clone of the original. Thus far, he's been murdered, resurrected in a new body and transported to another planet, but no worries—it's all good: Gosseyn's rigorous training in the mind-body coordination techniques of General Semantics has rendered him immune to trauma. All he needs to do is take a brief "cortico-thalamic pause," and he's ready to face the next bizarre plot twist. During the "pause," a Null-A elite is able to throw off all previous cultural programming and process new sense data from a serene perspective. Eventually, we find out that Gosseyn is actually a mutant, a breakthrough in human evolution, a superbeing with an "extra brain" who's being manipulated by the cosmic chess player in order to combat galactic conspirators who want to wipe out the General Semantics crowd and take over the universe. Got that, chillun'?

Wow, I thought, this is great, immediately realizing that this "cortico-thalamic pause" business could serve as a psychological defense against Parent-Things, Teacher-Things and Life-Things in general. Moreover, like Gilbert Gosseyn, I could be a good mutant and combat the forces of evil throughout the galaxy. But how do I get the training? There was no Institute of General Semantics. It was just something out of A. E. van Vogt's imagination.

Wrong, little Donny. If I'd just done a bit of research, I would've found out that a very real Institute of General Semantics was housed in a country estate in Lime Rock, Connecticut, a few hours' drive from Kendall Park. It seems that van Vogt was using his novel to illustrate his greatest intellectual passion: the system of General Semantics as described in *Science and Sanity*, a very thick book by a jaunty Polish aristocrat, Count Alfred Korzybski.

After serving in the Polish army during World War I, Korzybski decided that people had better find a way to get along with each other. Of course, the same idea had generated

Communism, Fascism, Anarcho-Syndicalism and a hundred other political isms. The Count, though, saw all problems in human relations as problems in semantics, that is, the fact that words mean different things to different people. Moreover, *General* Semantics, his own invention, would also take into account neurological events: the ways in which people reacted to new words, new information and new situations. Confronted with a stressful stimulus, one's reflexes and/or conditioned behavior often preempted the appropriate measured response.

Korzybski wondered whether there was a way to align the cortex, the part of the brain that has dominion over rational thought, and the thalamus, the seat of emotions (hence van Vogt's cortico-thalamic pause). For starters, people had to change the way they perceived and evaluated the world around them. Rather than employ Aristotelian logic—that is, the binary, yes/no, black versus white type of thinking—the Count favored multivalued, pluralistic thought that was modulated by—but not ruled by—subjective feeling. Basically, Korzybski was saying, Hey, be cool: "Don't get mad—get Null-A!"

One of the Count's most quoted sentences is "The map is not the territory." In other words, don't confuse the word with the object, the description with the thing itself. People who want to sell you something intentionally take advantage of this confusion. For instance, political speeches, TV commercials and Fox News use language rife with "truthiness" instead of truth and contain "factoids" rather than facts.

General Semantics also advances the concept of time-binding: the fact that humans can leave books and recordings and films to transmit knowledge to successive generations gives them an enormous evolutionary advantage, one that mustn't be squandered. Then there's the related concept of abstraction: when we see an event, we never see its essence, but abstract just a slice of the whole. In order to make use of this knowledge, the Count believed that one must be reeducated to process information with an open mind, with a minimum of unhealthy ego and in a spirit of cooperation, not competition. Although he suggests a number of different learning techniques, one of the most important tools was a discussion group that was part seminar and part group therapy. If you were lucky, the group leader was the Count himself.

If this is starting to remind you of any number of human-potential movements that sprung up during the latter part of the twentieth century, it's no accident. The editor of *Astounding Science Fiction*, John W. Campbell, the man whose vision ushered in the "golden age" of science fiction, was obsessed with the Nietzschean concept that called for a class of supermen at the top of the social hierarchy. When Campbell read Korzybski's book, he envisioned Null-A training as the first step to some sort of actual über-mutancy, and urged his team of writers, including Robert Heinlein, Lester del Rey, L. Sprague de Camp and van Vogt, to work the concept into their stories. Another of his *Astounding* writers, L. Ron Hubbard, had an even better idea: he co-opted some of the Count's more accessible ideas, threw in some basic Freud, and wrote *Dianetics*. In 1950, the charismatic Hubbard even convinced his old pal van Vogt to run his California Dianetics operation. The two pulp writers had a falling-out when Hubbard, dismayed by diminishing sales figures, sweetened the deal by coming up with Scientology, a fanciful, sci-fi religion.

Many well-intentioned psychologists have acknowledged a debt to General Semantics: Fritz Perls (Gestalt therapy, Esalen), Albert Ellis (cognitive therapy) and Neuro-Linguistic Programmers Richard Bandler and John Grinder were all heavy Korzybski-ites. So were Buckminster Fuller, S. I. Hayakawa, Alvin Toffler, anthropologist Gregory Bateson, philosopher Alan Watts, literary theorist Kenneth Burke, and the originator of *The Tonight Show*, Steve Allen (*smock-smock!*). Additional science fiction writers who were influenced by General Semantics and/or A. E. van Vogt: Frank Herbert, Philip K. Dick (very big on amnesiac mutants), Arthur C. Clarke, Harlan Ellison, Robert Anton Wilson, Poul Anderson, Philip José Farmer and many more. In recent years, a new generation of sci-fi writers has been exploring the latest pimp-my-human movement. It's known as Transhumanism and has a logo every bit as snappy as Null-A: H+.

After *Science and Sanity* became a runaway hit with the egghead crowd, in 1938 the Count established the Institute of General Semantics in Chicago (it moved to Connecticut in 1946). In attendance at his summer lecture series of 1939 was Harvard student William S. Burroughs, the future writer of *Junkie, Queer, Naked Lunch* and other works. Several of the core concepts that Burroughs would preach to his flock—the idea that language is a virus, the routine about the "IS of identity" and the "EITHER/OR" problem—certainly had their origins in General Semantics. So if we are alert to the fact that Burroughs was an idol of both J. G. Ballard and William Gibson, we can trace Null-A's influence back through three generations of sci-fi greats.

A note: In the mid-sixties, Burroughs joined the Church of Scientology and was a member until 1972 when, disgusted with Hubbard's increasingly megalomaniacal statements and behavior, he moved on to higher ground, so to speak. Apparently, he was still quoting Korzybski through his last days.

I never did get the hang of that cortico-thalamic pause or grow golden tendrils out of my head like the mutants in van Vogt's other classic, *Slan*. It seemed that, if you wanted to go mutant, you had to be born into a family of superhumans or join a political group or a religion. And the truth was, I was never much of a joiner.

2

In September 1966, when I was a student at Bard College, my formerly tweedy, graying poetry professor, Anthony Hecht, showed up for the new term in gray-and-white-striped Uncle Sam bell-bottoms, a bright paisley shirt, a suede vest and Beatle boots. My friends and I discovered that these, along with a new laid-back, goofy expression, were the souvenirs of a summer spent among the flower children of Haight-Ashbury, a section of San Francisco that was just starting its climb to glory. Of course, we had to check it out as well. So, a few months later, a few of us drove out to the coast.

The scene, made eerily vivid by the combination of psychedelic drugs and its own outrageous novelty, was pure science fiction: all these dazzling young girls dressed up in homemade outfits inspired by Pocahontas, Maid Marian, Annie Oakley, whoever. Tall, bony drug dealers with ponytails would walk past you muttering the names of their wares without the vow-els, just in case you were a narc: *Hsh!—Grss!—Zd!—Spd!* Blue Cheer, a group that touted itself as the loudest band in the world, was playing down the street at the Straight Theater.

It was fascinating, for about a week, anyway. Then you started to notice that a lot of the kids looked all waxy and wild-eyed and that they were talking much too slow or much too fast, and then you got that *Oh shit* feeling like Lou Costello thinking he's talking to Abbott and then realizing he's talking to the Wolfman. On the corner, you'd spot the hustling predator (whose consciousness hadn't been raised as yet) looking to score off the middle-class kids who'd walked right onto their turf. It was over, bro, before it even hit *Life* magazine.

By 1968, the paranoia was thick. The Vietnam War was esca-lating, Kennedy II and King were assassinated, and both the right and the left were caught in a cycle of fear and fury. Sev-eral gruesome murders (the "Groovy" murders, Manson) broke the spirit of the alternative community. Almost immedi-ately, the counterculture, this alliance of aspiring mutants, seemed to have a nervous breakdown and fragmented into claques devoted to one authority figure or another: you could sign up with the Maharishi, Meher Baba, Rajneesh and his Orange People, Sun Myung Moon, the Sufis, the Jesus Freaks, the Hare Krishnas and various sects of Buddhists. In addition, there were the human-potential movements already men-tioned, plus EST, Arica, primal therapy and scores of others. In the political sphere, you had the Panthers and the Weather-men. All this provided me and my droll companions with a lot of great material for after-dinner analysis, with or without herbal mood augmentation. Not that we all weren't feeling a little shaky ourselves. Now everyone had a map, but, as the Count liked to say, the map is not the territory. After a while, there wasn't any territory, either.

3

There were a few SF writers, like antiauthoritarian satirists Frederik Pohl and C. M. Kornbluth, who wouldn't buy into John Campbell's dream of a mutant utopia. In the early fifties, when Philip K. Dick tried to sell Campbell a story about a postatomic mutant—a perfect being who turns out to have no use for the human race—Campbell wouldn't allow it. Dick's comments:

> Here I am also saying that mutants are dangerous to us ordinaries, a view which John W. Campbell, Jr., deplored. We were supposed to view them as our leaders. But I always felt uneasy as to how they would view us. I mean, maybe they wouldn't want to lead us. Maybe from their superevolved lofty level we wouldn't seem worth leading. Anyhow, even if they agreed to lead us, I felt uneasy as to where we would wind up going. It might have something to do with build ings marked SHOWERS but which really weren't.

Predictably, Campbell thought Dick's stories were "not only worthless, but nuts"; Dick, as much as he enjoyed van Vogt, eventually came to see both Campbell and his pal Heinlein as dangerous right-wing loonies.

In the same anthology that contained "The Father-Thing," there was a complete novel, *The Stars My Destination*, by Alfred

Bester, a young, hip Manhattanite who also wrote for radio, comics, the slicks and early TV. In 1953, "Alphie" Bester won the very first Hugo Award for his novel *The Demolished Man*, a dark tale of a powerful, wealthy man who is defeated by his own self-annihilating Id. These two novels (as well as some terrific stories) were distinguished by a manic style and an arch urban humor that were not lost on the cyberpunkers to come.

Like most of Campbell's young colleagues, Bester idolized him, though they'd never actually met. Shortly after Bester sent Campbell a few stories, the great man called and asked him to come into the office to talk about some changes. Bester was psyched. Being more of a midtown gent (or more naïve) than most of the geeks in the field, Bester was astonished when the "editorial offices" of *Astounding Science Fiction* turned out to be a small, scuzzy room in the bowels of an industrial printing plant out in Jersey. Campbell told Bester he liked one of his stories, but was unhappy that the main character's behavior was driven by unconscious, "Freudian" impulses. Years later, Bester described the conversation:

"You don't know it," Campbell said, "you can't have any way of knowing it, but Freud is finished . . . destroyed by one of the greatest discoveries of our time."
"What's that?"
"Dianetics."
"I never heard of it."
"It was discovered by L. Ron Hubbard and he will win the Nobel peace prize for it," Campbell said solemnly.
"The peace prize? What for?"

"Wouldn't the man who wiped out all war win the Nobel peace prize?"

Campbell then handed Bester the galley proofs of Hubbard's first Dianetics piece, which was to appear in the next issue of *Astounding*, and told him to read it. Afterward, he took Bester downstairs to the printer's cafeteria for lunch, where, then and there, Campbell tried to "clear" him of his "engrams" (emotional blockages). Desperately trying not to laugh, Bester finally begged off, explaining that his emotional wounds were too much to bear. He raced back to the city and consoled himself with "three double Gibsons."

While it's true that Bester's plots tended to follow a psycho-analytic model—which is another way of describing classical heroic tragedy—he never seemed to care much for systems or politics. His self-made supermen are lone wolves, and their rebirth is always acquired by trial and error, and at great cost. Gully Foyle, the brutish protagonist of *The Stars My Destination* doesn't have a clan or a training manual to help him on his journey toward cosmic destiny; all he has to work with is his rage at the Vorga, the passing cruiser that left him to perish after being shipwrecked in deep space. In Bester's twenty-fifth century, there's nothing like a tradition of General Semantics to hold society together. People are as they've ever been: greedy and impulsive, vicious, self-interested, loving and scattered. Here is Bester's mock-Dickensian prologue:

This was a Golden Age, a time of high adventure, rich living, and hard dying . . . but nobody thought so. This was a future of fortune and theft, pillage and rapine, culture and vice . . . but nobody admitted it. This was an age of extremes, a fascinating century of freaks . . . but nobody loved it . . .

All the world was misshapen in marvelous and malevolent ways. The Classicists and Romantics who hated it were unaware of the potential greatness of the twenty-fifth century. They were blind to a cold fact of evolution . . . that progress stems from the clashing merger of antagonistic extremes, out of the marriage of pinnacle freaks. Classicists and Romantics alike were unaware that the solar system was trembling on the verge of a human explosion that would transform man and make him the master of the universe.

Back in my room, in Kendall Park, reading by the light of a tensor lamp, I thought: he's describing the twenty-fifth century, but . . . maybe, out there somewhere, across Route 27, just around the next curve of space-time, the second half of the twentieth century might be just as exciting—even though nobody thinks so. The remarkable technologies, intrepid spacers walking on the moon, the loud, wild music, the sex, the social and cultural upheavals, the colors, the freaks, the fun—in short, the adventure.

I Was a Spy
for Jean Shepherd

I was introduced to Shep, as his fans called him, by my weird uncle Dave. Dave, who was a bit of a hipster, used to crash on our sofa when he was between jobs. Being a bookish and somewhat imperious twelve-year-old, already desperately weary of life in suburbia and appalled by Hoss and Little Joe and Mitch Miller and the heinous Bachelor Father, I figured Dave was my man. One night, after ruthlessly beating me at rummy, he put down the cards and said, "Now we're gonna listen to Shepherd—this guy's great." The Zenith table radio in the kitchen came to life midway through Shepherd's theme music, a kitschy, galloping Eduard Strauss piece called the "Bahn Frei" polka. And then there was this voice, cozy, yet abounding with jest.

If you know Jean Shepherd's name, it's probably in connection with the now classic film *A Christmas Story*, which is based on a couple of stories in his book *In God We Trust: All Others Pay Cash*. He also did the compelling voice-over narration. Every Christmas, TBS presents a twenty-four-hour *A Christmas Story* marathon.

There are annual fan conventions devoted to the film— released thirty years ago this Thanksgiving—and the original location, a house in Cleveland, has been turned into a museum. But long before *A Christmas Story* was made, Shepherd did a nightly radio broadcast on WOR out of Manhattan that enthralled a generation of alienated young people within range of the station's powerful transmitter. Including me: I was a spy for Jean Shepherd.

In the late fifties, while Lenny Bruce was beginning his climb to holy infamy in jazz clubs on the West Coast, Shepherd's all-night monologues on WOR had already gained him an intensely loyal cult of listeners. Unlike Bruce's provocative nightclub act, which had its origins in the "schpritz" of the Catskills comics, Shepherd's improvised routines were more in the tradition of Midwestern storytellers like Mark Twain, but with a contemporary urban twist: say, Mark Twain after he'd been dating Elaine May for a year and a half. Where Bruce's antics made headlines, Shepherd, with his warm, charismatic voice and folksy style, could perform his most subversive routines with the bosses in the WOR front office and the FCC being none the wiser. At least, most of the time.

He was definitely a grown-up but he was talking to me—I mean straight to me, with my twelve-year-old sensibility, as if some version of myself with twenty-five more years worth of life experience had magically crawled into the radio, sat down and loosened his tie. I was hooked. From then on, like legions of other sorry-ass misfits throughout the Northeast, I tuned in every weeknight at eleven fifteen and let Shep put me under his spell. Afterwards, I'd switch to an all-night jazz station and dig the sounds until I conked out. Eventually, this practice started to affect my grades and I almost didn't graduate from high school.

Listening to Shep, I learned about social observation and human types; how to parse modern rituals (like dating and sports); the omnipresence of hierarchy; joy in struggle; "slobbism"; "creeping meatballism"; nineteenth-century panoramic painting; the primitive, violent nature of man; Nelson Algren, Brecht, Beckett, the fables of George Ade; the nature of the soul; the codes inherent in "trivia"; bliss in art; fishing for crappies; and the transience of desire. He told you what to expect from life (loss and betrayal) and made you feel that you were not alone.

Shepherd's talk usually fell into one of four categories. Fans of *A Christmas Story* will be familiar with the basic comic tone of his Depression-era tales, elaborations on his experience growing up in Hammond, Indiana, a Chicago suburb in the shadow of U.S. Steel on Lake Michigan. These stories featured his manic father ("the old man"), his mother (always standing over the sink in "a yellow rump-sprung chenille bathrobe with bits of dried egg on the lapel"), his kid brother, Randy, and assorted pals, bullies, beauties and other neighborhood types. While the film preserves much of the flavor of Shep's humor, not much remains of the acid edge that characterized his on-air performances. In the film, the general effect is one of bittersweet nostalgia. On the radio, the true horror of helpless childhood came through.

Then there were the stories culled from his three years in the stateside army during World War II (a juvenile ham radio and electronics freak, he was assigned to the Signal Corps). The third hunk of material was informed by his adventures in postwar radio and TV. He seems to have done every possible job, from engineer to sportscaster to hosting live cowboy music broadcasts. Finally, there was the contemporary stuff, comments on the passing scene.

In between, he'd sing along to noisy old records, play the kazoo and the nose flute, brutally sabotage the commercials and get his listeners—the "night people," the "gang"—to help him pull goofy public pranks on the unwitting squares that populated most of Manhattan. In one famous experiment in the power of hype, Shepherd asked his listeners to go to bookstores and make requests for *I, Libertine*, a nonexistent novel by a nonexistent author, Frederick R. Ewing. The hoax quickly snowballed and several weeks later *I, Libertine* was on bestseller lists. (Shep and sci-fi author Theodore Sturgeon eventually codged together an actual novel of that title for Ballantine Books. I owned a copy.)

Hilarious as Shep's tales could be, one sensed a tough realism about life that ran counter to the agitprop for the Leisure Revolution that the media were serving up in those years. With the Soviets flexing their muscles and the constant specter of global nuclear war, the government was going to fantastic lengths to convince everyone that things were just peachy. From Bert the Turtle's exhortations to "duck and cover" in the face of an atomic blast to the endless parade of new products hawked on the tube by Madison Avenue, Americans were feeding themselves a line of hooey that was no less absurd than the most hard-core Maoist brainwash. "Relax, life is good," we were told. "Your government and Walt Disney have got the future well in hand." To skeptical *Mad* magazine–reading little stinkers like myself, it was this mendacity on the part of adults that was the most sinister enemy of all.

Because Shep made it clear he was just as dazed, enraged and amused as you were, that he noticed what you noticed, he established himself as one of a handful of adults you could trust. (Others were Mailer, Ginsberg, Vonnegut and *Realist* publisher Paul Krassner.) Night after night, Shepherd forged the inchoate thoughts and feelings of a whole generation of fans into an axiom that went something like "The language of our culture no longer describes real life and, pretty soon, something's gonna blow."

Toward the beginning of the show, Shepherd frequently read news clippings that listeners, his "spies," had sent in. These were mostly odd little fillers he called "straws in the wind," indicators of the prevailing mood. Once I mailed Shep an article from our local Central Jersey paper about a guy who, after being fired for some petty infraction, got loaded and tossed a Coke bottle through every store window in the local shopping mall. A couple of nights later, I'm listening to the show and Shep does his usual bit: "So, this kid sent me a piece . . ." And he ACTUALLY READ MY CLIP ON THE AIR! *Wham*: I had connected. My life as an independent consciousness had begun. I remember scurrying down to the TV room and announcing this amazing event to my parents. Having always considered both Shepherd and my uncle Dave to be half-cracked, they were greatly underwhelmed.

As grateful as I am that Shep was there for me during those crucial years, my idealization of Shepherd the Man was not to survive much longer. In December 1965, I came home from my first year of college for Christmas break and noticed that Shepherd was going to be appearing at nearby Rutgers University.

On a frosty night, I drove my used Ford Galaxy to New Brunswick, where I sat on the floor with a congregation of Rutgers students and watched Shep walk into the spotlight to enthusiastic applause. He had neat but stylishly long hair and was wearing a green corduroy sports coat with the collar up over a black turtleneck tee.

Onstage for almost two hours, he had the young audience in his pocket from the downbeat. But, for me, something wasn't right. On the radio, speaking close to the mic, he was able to use vocal nuances and changes in intensity to communicate the most intimate shadings of thought and feeling, not unlike what Miles Davis could achieve in a recording studio. Live onstage, he spoke as though he'd never seen a microphone in his life, trying to project to the back of the room. Moreover, he blared and blustered like a carnival barker, as if he had the scent of failure in his nostrils and was ready to do anything to get the crowd on his side. It was obvious that the guy I thought was so cool had a desperate need to impress all these people, whom I assumed to be casual listeners at best.

In truth, even at home, listening on the radio, I'd noticed a strain of grandiosity creeping into Shepherd's routines. Apparently, he'd originally gone to New York with the idea of being a stage actor or making it big on network TV. But it's easy to imagine mainstream producers and network execs being put off by Shepherd's contrariness and intrinsic marginality. Supposedly, when Steve Allen retired as host of *The Tonight Show*, he'd suggested Shepherd as a replacement. NBC ended up giving the job to the eccentric but more cuddly Jack Paar. In any case, as the years rolled by, Shepherd rankled at being confined to the ghetto of radio and must have come to see his crown as King of the Hipsters as a crown of thorns.

What I saw that night at Rutgers wasn't pretty. In the studio, his occasional abuse of the lone engineer on the other side of the glass could be seen as the petulance of an artist trying to make things work on the fly. But, incandescent under the gaze of all those kids, his self-indulgences looked more like straight-up narcissism and his "hipness" was revealed as something closer to contempt. By the end of the show, he'd crossed the line between artist and showman and then some. No longer wanting to meet the great man, I left before the reception, scraped the ice off my windshield and drove home. Anyway, the cool early sixties were over and the boiling, psychedelic late sixties had begun. Shepherd was no longer part of my world.

Not long ago, in the absence of any books, films, music, and so on, that seemed to give off any light, I started looking back at some of the things that used to inspire me as a kid, including Shep's old shows, many of which are now available on the Internet. Hearing them almost a half century down the line has been a trip. Despite the tendencies I've already mentioned (plus the gaffes one might expect from a wild man like Shep ad-libbing before the age of political correctness), much of the stuff is simply amazing: the guy is a dynamo, brimming with curiosity and ideas and fun. Working from a few written notes at most, Shepherd is intense, manic, alive, the first and only true practitioner of spontaneous word jazz.

I've done a little catch-up research: Shepherd stayed on at WOR until 1977, when the station did a makeover. His books, collections of stories based on the same material he used on the air, sold well. He had a successful career on public television and continued to do his bit onstage into the nineties. And, of course, there was the collaboration with director Bob Clark on *A Christmas Story*. But I'm sorry to report that the narcissism thing kept getting worse as he got older.

Like a lot of fine-tuned performing artists, Shepherd increasingly exhibited the whole range of symptoms common to the aging diva. He became paranoid and resentful of imagined rivals, whether they were old ones like Mort Sahl or upstarts like Garrison Keillor. At the same time, he disavowed all his radio work, claiming that it was just a temporary gig on his way to some fanciful glory on the stage and screen. He even seemed to want to kill off his childhood, insisting that all those stories and characters were pulled clear out of his imagination. Old fans, for whom he had been almost like a surrogate father or big brother, were often met with derision when they approached him.

He didn't drink himself to death like his pal Jack Kerouac or OD like Lenny Bruce, but gradually succumbed to that very real disease of self-loathing and its accompanying defenses. Disappointed in the way the world had treated him, he retired to Florida's west coast and died in 1999.

Although Shepherd almost never divulged details about his private life, he wasn't shy about giving us a bit of unflattering self-analysis, as this fragment of a show from 1957 attests:

Protective coloration is extremely important in our lives . . .
We are in the weeds all the time because we find it better
down here in the weeds . . . Look at me . . . I am not at all what
I appear to be . . . This is merely a mask . . . that more or less

covers up the real me that's underneath. The real me is a saber-toothed tiger. I couldn't dare go down the street the way I really am. I'd get shot in five minutes. They'd have me in a wagon with a bunch of Doberman pinschers.

To an adolescent back then, long before a therapeutic vernacular had entered the language, this was reassuring news. It's possible that Shep's greatest lesson to the gang wasn't just "Things are not what they seem" but rather "Things are not what they seem—including me."

In the Clubs

I started going to jazz clubs in New York when I was twelve or thirteen, first with my older cousins Mike and Jack, and then later on my own. I remember seeing the mighty Count Basie band at a matinee at Birdland, with the great Sonny Payne on drums. When the whole band pumped out one of those thirteenth chords, you could feel the breeze on your face.

Once upon a time, the jazz club was a mythic place that signified urban romance, free-loving hipsterism and the Dionysian rites of the Exotic Black Man: in short, the dread possibility of ecstasy. As a survivor of many nights in actual jazz clubs, I can testify that the image was only partly correct.

Like most of the finer things in life, jazz is an acquired taste. As a suburban youth, I would often ride the bus up the New Jersey Turnpike through the industrial wasteland that must be crossed before the island of Manhattan is won. The combined sum of several weeks' allowance would be burning a hole in my pocket. After docking at the dependably sinister Port Authority terminal, I'd take the AA train to Waverly Place in the West Village, which by then had pretty much completed its transformation from bohemia into Bohemia Land. Tourists nursed espressos at the Cafe Wha? and the Cafe Bizarre. At

Figaro's coffee shop on Bleecker and MacDougal, I'd order a burger and listen to my heart pound as I watched the exquisite, joyless waitresses slink around the room in black leotards. An epigraph on the menu read "Where the Beat meet the Elite."

By the early sixties, jazz, having already been displaced as America's dance music of choice by rock and roll, was facing another crisis. College kids, after a brief flirtation with bop and cool jazz, had chosen "folk" music as their official enthusiasm. Unlike gnarly post-Parker jazz, guitar-based roots music was totally accessible and irony free, and almost anyone could play it in some form. Moreover, the leftist anthems of the Depression were easily adapted to become the official music of the early civil rights movement. New clubs featuring Dylan, The Tarriers, Judy Collins, Richie Havens, and the like were pulling in a huge share of the business. Nevertheless, the Village was still the best place to hear jazz in its last glorious incarnation.

At the Village Vanguard, my distress at being the youngest person in the audience would dissolve as soon as the music started. In the early sixties, gods stood on that tiny stage. A lot of them drank J&B and smoked Luckies, but they were gods just the same. Miles Davis, Sonny Rollins and John Coltrane were still youngish, fearless and working at the summit of their creativity. The proprietor, Max Gordon, once he got to know my face, used to seat me at the banquet next to the drum kit and give me a flat bar Coke. The cover charge was, like, seven bucks.

One of my favorites was bassist/composer Charles Mingus, who'd always bring along his demonic drummer, Dannie Richmond. Every time Richmond started banging out that triple time, the vibration of his sizzle cymbal would move my glass toward the edge of the table and I'd have to push it back to the center. I remember Mingus halting a tune in midgallop to lecture us on race, politics, cheating record companies and hypocrisy, both black and white. Watching this tempestuous artist at work, I found the extramusical events just as exciting as the music. I have to admit cringing, though, when Mingus, on one of his rougher nights, started screaming "Uncle Tom!" at old Coleman Hawkins, who was sitting at the bar. Hawk just gave him a world-weary smile and took another swig. Once, when I complimented pianist Jaki Byard after a set, he actually sat down at my table and graciously answered some questions about the music.

As the premier club in New York at that time, the Vanguard attracted a crowd that was a mix of serious fans and tourists. Of course there would always be the young preppie in a blazer sitting with his date, attractive in a little black dress. Imagine a split-screen: On the left, the kid's eyes are wide, his face is flushed; he's transfixed. He can't believe he's finally in a real jazz club twelve feet away from the great John Coltrane, who's blowing up a hurricane.

His date, on the right side of the screen, is in hell. Although she's heard her boyfriend talk about jazz, this is her first real exposure. She's been in this tiny, smoky, smelly room for almost an hour now, nursing screwdrivers and being forced to listen to four Negroes create a din that sounds like nothing imagined on God's earth. She's got her head in her hands down on the table because it hurts, a real pounder behind the eyes. Most humiliating is the fact that her boyfriend has forsaken her for a black man who seems to be using his silver horn as a satanic instrument of masturbation. The two sides of the screen merge when she finally pulls on her date's arm and demands to be escorted out. In the clubs, this classic scene can still be glimpsed today, always interesting, always poignant.

Two of the most mind-blowing musicians I got to see at the Vanguard were both patriarchs of early jazz who were still active in the sixties. Earl "Fatha" Hines had been a member of Armstrong's original Hot Five and, during the thirties, had been the main attraction at Al Capone's Grand Terrace Ballroom in Chicago. As if that weren't enough, the band he'd led in the forties, the one that included Charlie Parker, Dizzy Gillespie, Gene Ammons and Wardell Gray, was the first big band to feature bebop players and arrangements. Hines's gold lamé jacket, legendary smile and many-ringed fingers had the same effect on me as I'm sure they had on the crowd at the Grand Terrace. And then he began to play. I pretty much knew what to expect: he still played clean and swinging. I suppose it was my romantic imagination, but the music seemed to be enhanced by a sonic glow, an aura earned on its journey across an ocean of time.

The same could be said of the music of Willie "The Lion" Smith. In the twenties and thirties, Willie had been one of the mighty virtuosos who developed Harlem "stride" piano. In the sixties, Willie was still sharp and strong, a past master who seemed to have walked straight from a Depression rent party into the present, complete with cocked derby, milk bottle glasses and clenched cigar. He'd worked up his act into a seminar in jazz history, alternating pieces from his repertoire with stories about the musical life of Harlem, the cutting contests, the gangsters and the nuances that defined the styles of his contemporaries James P. Johnson, Fats Waller, Luckey Roberts and

Eubie Blake. He had a special affection for his protégé Duke Ellington, whose works he generously performed.

Claiming that his father was a Jewish gambler, Willie peppered his tales with Yiddishisms and made a point of wearing a Jewish star. Though the jive was fascinating, the real fun began when he commenced his abuse of the Steinway, his phenomenal left hand pumping like a locomotive as the right filigreed the melody. After knocking out his version of "Carolina Shout," Willie's comment was "Now that's what you call . . . *real good.*" But he could be lyrical too, as he was on his own "Echoes of Spring."

One more thing about the tough, road-hardened African American entertainers from the twenties who had to be heard without the benefit of microphones, men like Willie, Earl Hines, Coleman Hawkins, Ellington's band: they could play *REALLY LOUD!*

Bill Evans at the Vanguard was always a gas. Those familiar only with his studio recordings don't realize what a spry, funky hard-charger he could be on "up" material in a live setting. When he played quirky tunes like "Little Lulu," he could be funny, too. Of course, even then, he rarely shifted out of that posture you see in photos, doubled over at the waist, head inside the piano as if trying to locate a rattly string. By the late seventies, I noticed that this quintessential modernist had developed an odd, loping shuffle in his right-hand lines, as if he was regressing to an antiquated rhythmic style dating back to Willie Smith's day. What was up with that?

Real fans and serious hipsters remember Slug's Bar on Third Street between avenues B and C. The neighborhood was dicey but the sounds were happening. Some nights, the audience would be just me, eyes darting around nervously, and maybe two heavily medicated patrons nodding at their tables. Cedar Walton, Jackie McLean, Art Farmer and Jimmy Cobb were among the regular performers. In 1972, trumpet star Lee Morgan's girl shot and killed him out front.

Around 1965, the folk/rock club Cafe au Go Go started a Monday night jazz policy. These were jam sessions featuring top players who happened to be in town. The one I attended was one of the best all-around nights of jazz I ever saw. The rhythm section alone—Wynton Kelly on piano, Paul Chambers on bass and Willie Bobo on drums—began the set. The other players—Hank Mobley on tenor, Dave Pike on vibes and Curtis Fuller, I think, on bone—fell by as the night went on. Jamming on standards and blues for over two hours without a break, Mobley and Kelly were monstrous: hard-swinging and composing in the moment. It was the shit and I knew I was lucky to be there.

When the civil rights movement became more militant in the mid-sixties, the music followed suit. In those years, a lot of jazz was motivated by righteous political fury, or directed toward a spiritual catharsis. The clubs, overwhelmed for the moment by the rock revolution, began to close. The Five Spot, the Half Note and, finally, Slug's, all gradually vanished. The Village Gate managed to survive only by switching to rock and Latin sounds.

In the eighties, the jazz scene returned, "healthier" than ever. You'd go to hear acts in nifty, wholesome "club environments" and "art spaces." No smoking, of course, no nodding junkies, no heavy boozing—in fact, no vice of any kind except, perhaps, the criminally high cover and drink charges. The clubs that presented the top mainstream acts all had a suitably mainstream look and were very strict about reservations. One night in the eighties, I took some friends to Michael's Pub, then home to Woody Allen's Monday night gigs, to see a piano trio. The atmosphere was tense and the maitre d' was rude—there was no romance at all.

We split before the set started. Bring back Slug's!

Uncle Mort

As I remember, Mort Fega's radio show Jazz Unlimited *came on at midnight and ended at five or six a.m. In order to escape my parents' wrath, I had to pull the radio under the covers. I'd usually drift off before the closing theme.*

The Nightfly character from my first solo album wasn't supposed to be a stand-in for any particular jazz DJ. But there were a few actual radio personalities of the time that went into the mix. In the early sixties, a number of Manhattan's powerful stations were blasting hard bop throughout the metropolitan area. If you knew where to find it, you could hear great jazz around the clock.

After school, I'd rush home to hear Riverside Radio's fabulously erudite Ed Beach. Ed's show, *Just Jazz*, would use its full two hours to focus on just one player, or even one aspect of a player's career. After playing a favorite cut culled from his fabulous record collection, he'd tell you details about the recording session and make witty asides, drawing you in with his classical actor's voice and diction. I remember a program devoted exclusively to Johnny Hodges's work with small groups in the forties and fifties. There was another that covered trumpeter

Blue Mitchell's work as a sideman. Ed was talking to fellow fanatics only: dabblers, keep out.

Jazz critics Dan Morgenstern and Martin Williams both had excellent jazz shows back then, and I remember a droll dude named R. D. Harlan on WNCN. After midnight, I could always tune in to WADO and hear King Pleasure sing DJ "Symphony Sid" Torin's wiggy theme song:

Play anything cool for me and my baby
We don't want to think we're listenin' to lazy
It's got to be Prez, Bird, Shearing or the Basie
The dial is set right close to eighty—
Let 'er roll . . .

On Friday nights, Sid was still doing remote broadcasts from Birdland ("The Jazz Corner of the World"!). I'd close the door to my room and blast live music by Basie and Mingus out of that little Zenith table radio. Unhappily, Sid, an important advocate of modern jazz since the early days of bop, was, by the mid-sixties, pegged the "jazz traitor" for switching to a mostly Latin and Afro-Cuban playlist.

My main man was WEVD's all-night DJ Mort Fega. Unlike Symphony Sid, whose growling hepcat routine seemed out of sync with the Kennedy era ("No, dahling, I'm not goin'a play Etta Jones tonight"), Mort had no jive persona to sell. He was laid-back, knowledgeable and forthright, the cool uncle you always wished you'd had. I looked forward to Mort's between-track commentary as much as to the music itself. With Red Garland's

"Mort's Report" playing softly in the background, Mort, with the grace and enthusiasm that reveals itself only in the most bona fide jazz lover, would carefully list every soloist and sideman.

In those days, giants, as jazz fans like to say, walked the earth. They also recorded quite frequently for labels like Prestige, Blue Note, Columbia and Impulse, and Mort played them all—Miles, Monk, Rollins, Mingus, Coltrane, Bill Evans and so on. But he also had his own, somewhat lesser known, personal favorites. One was Oliver Nelson, whose exquisite *Blues and the Abstract Truth* album he helped to popularize. I recall frequent playings of Kenny Dorham's "Sao Paulo" with Joe Henderson on tenor. And it was on Mort's show that I first heard the exhilarating jive tales of His Royal Hipness, Lord Buckley. Many of his over-the-top routines, recorded in the mid-fifties, still resonated with the times. In Buckley's Mahatma Gandhi bit, "The Hip Gan," Mr. Rabadee, the band contractor, asks Gandhi to tell him which one of the instruments he digs the most. The Hip Gan tells him that "the instrument, you ain't got here."

Mister Rabadee said, "Man, what are you sayin'? I got the doong-doong players, and the bang-bang players, and the leb-edee players, and the reed heads, and the lute heads, and every head that I could dig up that swing out of the jungle here and you tell me that the one you dig the most I ain't got here?"

Said, "Dat's right."

He said, "Well, sweet double hipness, great beloved non-stop beauty, straighten me—'cause I'm ready."

And The Hip Gan say, "That's right, that's right. Well,

here's the lick." He said, "Baby, the instrument of all India which I dig the music the most of, that swings my soul up in that great cathedral-head of beauty is the music of the . . ."

(scats) He said, ". . . the spinnin' wheel, baby."

(scats) . . . knock a little patch on the cat's pants . . .

(scats) . . . swing a coat on Grandma . . .

(scats) . . . get a little juice on the table . . .

(scats) . . . swang up, get a little circus money . . .

(scats) . . . He said, "The spinnin' wheel, baby. I hope I didn't . . . bring you down."

Mort also had his salty side. My partner, Walter Becker, also a huge fan, told me that he once heard Mort express his disdain for avant-gardist Albert Ayler by playing a minute of a cut and then halting it with needle-scraping finality. If Ayler's saxophonic rage seemed more justifiable to my eighteen-year-old self in 1966, I can also recall the urge to scrape something across my college roommate's face when he cranked up Ayler's "Ghosts" at one o'clock in the morning.

Shortly before Mort died in 2005, Walter and I had a gig in Palm Beach, Florida. Mort and his wife, Muriel, had been living there since 1986. To our astonishment, he came to the gig and gave us a nice write-up in his *Palm Beach Post* column. Afterwards, we hooked up. He was just as cool and steady as he'd sounded all those years earlier when he rode WEVD's signal through the swirling, bitter Northeastern night. Using the hoary but handy language of jazz, a stew of Pops, Prez, Bird, Diz, Yiddish and British, he said that if we had "eyes to get together," we should just "give him a schrei."

A Talk with
Ennio Morricone ━━━━━━━━━

During my high school years I'd ride into Princeton on Saturday after-
noons and watch foreign movies at the Garden Theatre, an art house.
The early and mid-sixties were great years for European films. On a
regular basis, the Garden ran masterpieces by Fellini, Antonioni, Truf-
faut and a slew of British films by John Schlesinger, Tony Richardson,
Karel Reisz, Joseph Losey and others. One weekend, intrigued by an
ad, I decided to go slumming at the crap theater in New Brunswick and
see an Italian-made western, A Fistful of Dollars. *This turned out to*
be some illin' shit, and the music, by Ennio Morricone, was hilarious.
So, when Premiere *asked me in 1989 to interview Morricone, I bought*
a little recorder and met him at his hotel in midtown Manhattan. His
English wasn't so hot, so we talked through his translator.

Fagen: Maestro, the picture I have of Italian filmmaking comes
   mainly from Fellini films like *8½* and *La Dolce Vita*. When
   you were scoring spaghetti westerns in the sixties, was the
   scene really swinging?
Morricone: La Dolce Vita focused on a small group of people who
   got up at eleven p.m. and lived at night. While I, then as now,

got up at five in the morning to compose and was asleep by nine in the evening.

Fagen: Your music has always had a life here in America apart from the films. In the past few years, though, your influence has surfaced in a lot of rock music and in the works of "avant-garde" composers. Why is this music from twenty-five-year-old Italian westerns the talk of the town?

Morricone: I don't know. You tell me.

Fagen: Well . . .

Morricone: But I have a hypothesis. When I begin a theme in a certain key, say, D minor, I never depart from this original key. If it begins in D minor, it ends in D minor. This harmonic simplicity is available to everyone.

Fagen: But isn't it true that the Leone films, with their elevation of mythic structures, their comic book visual style and extreme irony, are now perceived as signaling an aesthetic transmutation by a generation of artists and filmmakers? And isn't it also true that your music for those films reflected and abetted Leone's vision by drawing on the same eerie catalog of genres—Hollywood western, Japanese samurai, American pop and Italian opera? That your scores functioned both "inside" the film as a narrative voice and "outside" the film as the commentary of a winking jester? Put it all together and doesn't it spell "postmodern," in the sense that there has been a grotesque encroachment of the devices of art and, in fact, an establishment of a new narrative plane founded on the devices themselves? Isn't that what's attracting lower Manhattan?

Morricone: [*shrugs*]

Fagen: What about your use of unusual solo instruments? You've hired Zamfir, master of the pan flute. You've featured whistlers and the human voice. Do you hear a specific color when you watch a scene?

Morricone: When I write a passage, I find out who's available. If the violinist I want is out of town, I'll use, say, a great flute player who is on a day layover in Rome. Sometimes it's even simpler. In *The Mission,* the character in the film plays the oboe, so . . .

Fagen: After scoring so many films, it must be hard to come up with fresh ideas.

Morricone: I saw *The Untouchables* on Monday, I thought of the main theme in the cab back to the hotel and played it for De Palma on Tuesday.

Fagen: You've worked with many directors, each who must present a different set of problems for the composer. I have a list here. What was it like working for Bertolucci?

Morricone: Bellissimo!

Fagen: Pontecorvo?

Morricone: He is my old friend—*bellissimo!*

Fagen: John Boorman?

Morricone: Bellissimo!

Fagen: Terrence Malick?

Morricone: A man with bad luck but . . . *bello, bellissimo!*

Fagen: Roman Polanski?

Morricone: Bellissimo!

Fagen: Brian De Palma?

Morricone: Bellissimo!

Fagen: Leone?

Morricone: Bellissimo!

Fagen: Your scores for Leone in particular had a very sly humor. Will you be composing for any comic or semicomic films in the near future?

Morricone: If they offer. I can only choose from the films that are offered me.

Fagen: Maestro, are there days when you wish you were still playing the trumpet?

Morricone: The trumpet was exhausting. I have always wanted to compose.

Exit the Genius ▬▬▬▬▬▬▬▬▬

Our next subject is entitled to his customary introduction: Ladies and Gentlemen, the Genius . . . the Genius of Ray Charles!

When Ray Charles died in 2004, we came to the end of American culture as we had known it. By alchemically combining elements of the sacred and the secular—basic country blues, club blues, country-and-western music, black gospel, the bebop of Charlie Parker and the canon of American standards—Brother Ray, musically speaking, solved the mind-body problem.

Ray's first models were the slick, popular trios of Nat Cole and, especially, Charles Brown. After a brief period of mimicry, he shook off Brown's twee, club-style delivery and found his own confident physicality that combined the Chicago cool of Cole with the passion of the black Baptist church. In other words, he decided to be Ray Charles. This could not have been that obvious a move for an ambitious black entertainer in 1952. Ray brought soul out of the closet.

At a recording session on November 18, 1954, Ray famously hijacked a gospel tune and, as he used to put it, "replaced God with a woman." The result, "I Got a Woman"—followed by "Drown in My Own Tears," "Hallelujah I Love Her So," "What

I Say" and so many others—rescued a generation from the deadly, neurotic suppression of feeling that had afflicted the nation after World War II. Two years later, "I Got a Woman" appeared on Elvis Presley's first album. Elvis wasn't the white Ray Charles, though. Tennessee Williams, maybe, comes closer.

The Ray Charles Effect was not limited to popular music. Ray's big and small bands (Ray did the arrangements, singing each man his part) had a huge influence on the direction jazz was to take in the fifties, a movement the unimpressed French critic André Hodeir used to call the "funky hard-bop regression." Horace Silver, Count Basie's "atomic" band, Charles Mingus, every funky artist on Blue Note—they all owed Ray Charles. Quincy Jones was a Seattle teenager when Ray moved to that city in 1948:

> Ray showed up, and he was around sixteen years old [actually, Ray was at least eighteen by then] and . . . he was like God, you know! He had an apartment, he had a record player, he had a girlfriend, two or three suits. When I first met him, you know, he would invite me over to his place. I couldn't believe it. He was fixing his record player. He would shock himself because there were glass tubes in the back of the record player then, and the radio. And I used to just sit around and say, "I can't believe you're sixteen. You've got all this stuff going." Because he was like . . . a brilliant old dude, you know. He knew how to arrange and everything. And he . . . taught me how to arrange in braille, and the notes. He taught me what the notes were, because he understood.

Ray's soul revolution ran parallel to, and interacted with, the civil rights movement of the fifties and sixties. In the more militant seventies, the funk of James Brown and Sly Stone took over to provide a more obvious sound track. Ray's attempts to jump on the funkwagon were halfhearted. The new black sound was colder and right up in your face, based, in fact, on a smaller division of the beat.* James Brown, Isaac Hayes and Barry White seemed less interested in pleasing a woman than in collecting body parts. In contrast, Ray's sage interpretation of "America the Beautiful" (1972) was at once a taunt, a healing gesture and a blind man's dream of the Promised Land. Perhaps a eulogy as well. Ray's work, even in decline, was always wiser and subtler than that of the new breed. It was music for adults.

For me, though, and a generation of suburban boomers, Ray was the Professor of Desire, and "Georgia on My Mind"—square-ass backup singers and all—just may have been the most beautiful three minutes and thirty-nine seconds in all of twentieth-century music.

* Not unlike the complex relationship of bop to the jazz that preceded it.

The Devil and Ike Turner

The general public, knowing little of Ike Turner's innovations as a player, producer and bandleader, seems more intrigued by his reputation as an iconic addict and wife-beater. But, by all accounts, Ike never even took a drink until he was in his thirties. Then he got lucky.

I got to keep movin'
I got to keep movin'
Blues fallin' down like hail
(Blues fallin' down like hail)
And the days keeps on worryin' me
There's a Hellhound on my trail
(Hellhound on my trail)
—Robert Johnson

Most all the musicians of my acquaintance know the legend of Robert Johnson, the great Delta bluesman. At a crossroads at midnight, Robert meets the devil (or Eshu or Papa Legba) and, in exchange for his immortal soul, comes away with supernatural skills as a singer and guitarist. Many versions of this Faustian story put the crossroads at Clarksdale, Mississippi, where Highway 49 meets Highway 61.

Muddy Waters was raised in Clarksdale. John Lee Hooker and Sam Cooke were born and grew up there. Ike Turner was a Clarksdale boy, too. This was the 1930s in the Deep South. Real bad stuff happened. Nevertheless, by the time he was a teenager, Ike could bang out a boogie on the piano and play the guitar with an authentic Delta twang. But in truth, talented as he was, there wasn't anything really supernatural about Ike's skills as a musician. His singing was always spirited, but, relative to the wealth of local competition, no big deal. What Ike excelled at was leadership: conceptualization, organization and execution. It's intriguing to think: if Ike walked down to the crossroads one moonless night, what exactly did he ask for?

Long before he met Tina (originally Anna Mae Bullock) in St. Louis in the late 1950s and began the sixteen-year partnership that would end with his name used mainly as a comic byword for "blow-addicted megalomaniacal black wife-beater," Ike had already been successful at some half dozen careers in music. He was a DJ, a relentless talent scout, an arranger (for Sam Phillips at Sun, among others), a bandleader (with his own group, the Kings of Rhythm) and a session player (he recorded with B.B., Howlin' Wolf, Elmore James and many others). His employers included the Bihari brothers at Modern Records, the Chess brothers in Chicago and a host of tough club owners. They didn't like to fool around with their money. Ike had to be at that session on time, he had to book those gigs, make sure the band's suits were pressed and that they rolled into the next town ready to play. Organization!

Ike could make things happen. Take "Rocket 88," a jump

blues tune about an Oldsmobile, which Ike and his Kings of Rhythm recorded in 1951. Chess Records released it under the name Jackie Brenston and His Delta Cats (Brenston, Ike's bari sax player, was the vocalist that day). A lot of music critics seem to think it was the first record to make the leap from R&B to rock and roll, probably because the busted amp that guitarist Willie Kizart was using added some serendipitous distortion to his sound. But it's Ike's stomping piano that drives the tune. "Rocket 88" went to number one on the R&B charts and, no doubt, Little Richard and Jerry Lee Lewis were listening.

The next year, the Bihari brothers sent him to Memphis to find bluesman Rosco Gordon. Ike liked Gordon's tune "No More Doggin'" and had Rosco bring in his band for a session. In fact, Ike liked the tune so much, he secretly had the band come back and record it again with himself singing. (Fortunately, Rosco heard what was going on and broke up Ike's game.) "No More Doggin'" made it to number two on the charts that year. Rosco Gordon's piano style—particularly on that record—was a quirky sort of boogie with a deep shuffle and a heavy accent on the upbeats. If it sounds almost like ska music when you hear it, it's no accident: the record is often cited as the template for Jamaican ska rhythm—whence came rock steady, whence came reggae. No wonder Ike tried to steal it.

When Papa Legba, the Crossroads Devil, steered Anna Mae Bullock into his path, Ike found his muse. I love all those early singles Ike worked up for Tina and the Ikettes: "A Fool in Love," "I Idolize You," "I Think It's Gonna Work Out Fine" and so on. Ike's concept (really a more raw and countrified version of Ray Charles's act) was simple: the band plays tight; Tina goes berserk. My favorite from this period, though, is "I'm Blue (The Gong-Gong Song)" by the Ikettes, with Dolores Johnson singing the lead vocal, a performance that actually justifies the overused term "kick-ass." A static sequence of stylized, transparent cells, this piece is Ike's overarching masterpiece (most people might be familiar with it as the sample used by Salt-N-Pepa in their 1993 hit "Shoop"). In 1965, Ike hired young Jimi Hendrix as a second guitarist for the Revue, but he was a big show-off, and Ike had to let him go: Jimi wouldn't stay inside the lines.

Papa Legba started to work overtime on Ike's behalf in the late sixties. Ike and Tina opened for the Stones and crossed over big-time by covering rock tunes like "Proud Mary" and "Honky Tonk Woman." Now they were superstars and the greenbacks were flowing. As is usual in these cases, Legba closed in to collect the vig. By all accounts, Ike got higher every year, and meaner, too. It's really hard to focus when there's a Hellhound on your trail. From Ike's point of view, squinting through the harsh fallout from all that booze and goofy dust, he may have figured that forceful action needed to be taken to ensure that everything in his world was up to his rigidly high standards of organization. He may have determined that, with the Hound so close and all, he'd better at least have his ducks in a row. Chaos had to be fended off, and the ends justified the means. Or something like that.

Or was it that Legba had given Ike exactly what he'd wished for—a schoolboy's dream of a girl who could be both a soul mate and a creature he could mold into the perfect lover and musical partner—knowing that Ike would never have the empathetic chops to see what he actually had? Ike had been programmed to blow it with Tina from the git-go.

After Tina finally left in 1976, Ike, already way shredded from the whole sex, drugs and rock 'n' roll thing, totally came apart. Years of continued heavy drug use and run-ins with the law ensued, culminating in his serving seventeen months in a California state prison. He was still in jail when he got the news that he and Tina had been inducted into the Rock and Roll Hall of Fame. Finally, just when things were starting to look up, Tina's book came out, followed by the film *What's Love Got to Do with It*.

Now the poster boy for spousal abuse, Ike started to fight his way back. He reconstituted the Kings of Rhythm and came out with a book of his own, *Takin' Back My Name* ("Sure, I've slapped Tina . . . We had fights and there have been times when I punched her without thinking . . . But I never beat her . . . I did no more to Tina than I would mind somebody doing to my mother in the same circumstances"). Obviously, there was something Ike just didn't get about the whole hitting problem. In his comeback shows, he had a series of surrogate Tinas come out in Tina-type outfits and sing Tina's songs. It seemed like he still couldn't figure out why she was gone. And yet he soldiered on, releasing two respectable albums, the second of which, *Risin' with the Blues*, won a Grammy in 2006.

How did Ike make out with the Crossroads Devil? We'll never know. Faust, in Goethe's version, does horrible things, especially in regard to his honey, Gretchen. At the end, he's about to be thrown into the yawning jaws of hell when a posse of angels comes to the rescue, singing:

He's escaped, this noble member
Of the spirit world, from evil

Whoever strives in his endeavor,
We can rescue from the devil.
And if he has Love within,
Granted from above,
The sacred crowd will meet him
With welcome, and with love.

I'd like to think Ike's version came out the same.

Class of '69 ▬▬▬▬▬▬▬▬▬▬▬▬▬▬▬▬

In his teens, my cousin Richard Cohn was an amateur magician. All of us kids would freak out when he'd perform at our birthday parties, pulling rabbits out of hats and coins out of our ears. (Later, he became a playwright and illustrator and changed his name to Dalt Wonk.) Since he seemed to prosper during his four years at Bard College, I applied as well. I must have been accepted on the basis of the great personal charm I displayed during my interview, because my high school grades sucked.

Situated on the lush east bank of the Hudson River just north of Rhinebeck, New York, Bard College was built on the former estate of its founder, John Bard, who'd wanted to establish a finishing school for Episcopalian ministers. By the 1960s, Bard had drifted, somewhat, from its theological origins. Now an infamous "progressive" school, it attracted a strange mix of applicants ranging from desperate suburban misfits with impressive verbal skills but appalling high school records (like myself) to pink-cheeked, short-sleeved-shirt-wearing "churchys" who were looking forward to contemplative nature walks and French horn sonatas in Bard Hall. There were private-school girls from Long Island and Connecticut in tennis whites, "red diaper" babies from Manhattan and a small contingent of droll, perpetually baked hipsters from the D.C. area. In 1965, Bard's student body numbered about six hundred students, total. There were no fraternities.

On a dark, drizzly morning, the first day of school, my father and I loaded up the trunk of his Olds Dynamic 88 in preparation for the drive to upstate New York. When he turned on the ignition, the Top 40 station was featuring "Like a Rolling Stone." That morning, we'd had a nasty argument when he'd refused to let me drive up alone in my own car. Feelings were still raw. Dylan's six-minute-plus majestic rant seemed, somehow, to validate my adolescent rage.

As the song played on (forever, it seemed), I looked over at my father sitting behind the wheel and couldn't help hearing the music through his ears. I was certain that what he was hearing wasn't a latter-day Beat masterpiece; it wasn't music or poetry at all, just self-indulgent noise. I couldn't help giggling to myself when I thought of a then recent *Mad* magazine parody that announced the release of a new album: *Bob Dilly Sings—Almost*. I was leaving one world, but hadn't quite arrived in the next.

Three tense hours later, we arrived on campus. Though the college had converted two elegant riverside manor houses into dormitory space, my own dorm was part of Stone Row, a group of ivy-covered buildings at the campus center in serious need of renovation. My father couldn't believe that Bard's exorbitant tuition (constituting the greater portion of his life savings) had bought me this dump of a room with leaky windows and peeling blue paint. Trying to make the best of it, he suggested to my roommate, a clarinetist named Chester Brezniak, that he toss a coin for the lower bunk. I won. I'm pretty sure my father cheated.

Two other students occupied tiny inner rooms. Lonnie was a senior, a painter with an outstanding record collection, an endless supply of marijuana and nightly visits from an assortment of willowy girlfriends. In the other room was Alan, a softspoken, Peter Pan–ish, coffee-colored dancer who was always wearing leg warmers. The thing was, as I'd never knowingly met a homosexual and had some doubt as to whether they actually existed, the only category I could think to put him in was, maybe, "hyperaesthetic messenger of the gods."

The first weekend after registration, flyers announced that there was to be a "tequila mixer" in Sottery Hall for the incoming class. Shortly before it was to begin, I happened to be in the court behind Stone Row when I saw a van skid into the main parking lot and disgorge a group of scuzzy hippies—actually, I don't think the word "hippy" was as yet being used to describe what they were—carrying guitars and equipment cases. This turned out to be the Group Image, an early tribal-type band that had been booked to provide the entertainment along with a fine band led by two Bardians, the Boylan brothers, called the Gingermen.

In high school, understand, I'd never had much of a social life. I was one of a few Jews in a spanking-new facility in rural New Jersey. Moreover, I was an introverted jazz snob who was afraid to ride in other kids' cars for fear that "Johnny Get Angry" by Joanie Sommers might come on the radio (though I did have a secret throb for Mary Weiss of the Shangri-Las). I tried taking up the baritone horn, but when the music teacher, Chauncey Chatten, forced me to march during halftime at football games, I gave the damn thing back. So, for most of my high school years, while the rest of my class was attending sports events or knocking over gas stations (I really had no idea what they did), I was home in my room flipping through the *Saturday Review* (I had a subscription), reading the thick Dover paperbacks I'd stolen from a basement bookshop in Princeton or sitting at the piano copping licks off Red Garland records. I didn't drink or smoke. Aside from Soupy Sales's rogue kiddie show, I had stopped watching TV when I was about thirteen. In short, I was a first-tier nerd, and pitifully lonely.

Lacking physical confidence, I was shy with girls. I'd skipped the proms and graduation and all that stuff. The idea of actually going on a date was both conceptually repugnant and beyond the limits of my courage. In my senior year, I'd somehow managed to gain the friendship of a gorgeous, sad and hilarious girl by tossing off snappy remarks. I could make her laugh, but it never went much further than that.

So I was a bit anxious when I walked into the Sottery Hall tequila mixer. The lights had been dimmed. Along one wall, several tables had been set up and stocked with hundreds of shot glasses rimmed with salt and filled with tequila. There were enormous wooden bowls of lemons and a fruit knife. After watching a few other students demonstrate their technique, I picked up a shot glass, bit into a lemon slice and threw the poison back.

A couple of hours and many shots later, I was sitting against a wall, unable to move, watching an extended jam by the Group Image. For whatever they may have lacked in the way of musical accomplishment, they compensated with real enthusiasm and some nice visuals, including a strobe lighting system—the first I'd ever seen—and a skinny girl singer named Sheila, who was wearing the shortest microskirt ever manufactured. She'd stopped singing early on and was now in a Dionysian trance, twitching like a maenad. That night, if I hadn't been paralyzed by the tequila, I would've tossed the whole college deal, crawled over to the band bus and begged them to take me with them, to whatever dissolute planet they were bound.

Of course, the next morning I postponed the call to adventure, vowed never again to drink the hard stuff and reverted back to young scholar. Though I'd dabbled in jazz piano and composing since I was a kid, I didn't think I had enough formal training to major in music, so I chose English, with a minor in heartbreak (more on that later). Bard was known for having a strong faculty and those years were no exception. I studied poetry with Anthony Hecht, philosophy with Heinrich Blücher and musical composition with Jacob Druckman. My favorite prof, though, was Baruch Hochman, a little Jewish firecracker and D. H. Lawrence freak with a brush mustache. He used to say things like "If all you do is identify with the protagonist, you're not fully engaged with the text—it's like making love to a woman and feeling nothing but your own body."

One overcast weekend in the spring of 1967, several of us participated in what turned out to be an underwhelming event called the "Human Be-In" in Central Park. Long-haired "freaks"—newly coined slang at the time—and their scrawny face-painted girlfriends ran around aimlessly while the Grateful Dead struggled in vain to get something going on a small jerry-built stage. The following morning, Hochman began class by looking around the room and saying, "I certainly

hope none of you attended that vulgar display in the park."
Silence prevailed.

I should comment on Bard's strangely apolitical character. After all, this was the sixties. I could say that the sort of student Bard attracted in those days, no matter from what background, tended to share that portion of the decade's ethos that was concerned with exploring inner space rather than the drive to interact with the world and effect change, or that we were in training to be cultural revolutionaries and not firebrands keen to man the barricades. I could say that the campus was isolated in a rural district that made access to daily newspapers and television difficult. But, folks, I don't want to be no jive turkey: most of us were just incredibly self-involved, happy as hell to be away from our "noids" (that's parents, from "paranoids") and primed to leave the repressive fifties behind and make the leap into the groovy, unbounded, sexualized Day-Glo future. The only demonstration I remember was a march on the president's house (totally justified) to protest the horrible quality of the food.

Besides, I had grave problems of my own. From the very first weeks at Bard, I'd fall in love with a new beauty at least once a semester, each one more unhinged than the last. Perhaps I felt more comfortable with girls who made me feel like my own degree of lunacy was less severe. But, if truth be told, I'd always been drawn to those damaged, incandescent originals who seemed to have, out of necessity, created themselves from scratch, whose core beauty reveals itself in the way they describe themselves and their world. In any case, there was certainly never any thought or calculation on my part. I'd spot someone in a class, or see a girl on the platform at Rhinecliff station, and that would be that.

Usually, I'd just stare at the object of desire from afar and die a thousand deaths. But not always. One numbing winter, I was so in love with a skipping blond pixie that I stopped eating and sleeping and developed walking pneumonia. I remember standing in the snow one night, tapping on her dorm window and pleading until she finally took me, coughing and weeping, into her bed. Another time, in the dining commons, I saw a tall, exotic creature in a ruffled miniskirt drop a slice of baloney on her slim, naked thigh, stare at it with an amused expression for a ten count, then peel it off and eat it. Years later, I looked her up and ended up following her to Paris.

Before the days of coed dorms, the enemies of romance were heartless men in heavy plaid jackets known as "proctors," official voyeurs whose job it was to roam the campus at night listening at windows for sounds of depravity. If they found a girl in a guy's dorm the slut was called out and marched back to her proper lodgings. Every so often I'd be awakened at four a.m. by the loud fulminations of a young swell defending the honor and identity of his giggling accomplice, refusing to give her up.

I actually made some friends at Bard, some of whom I'm still in touch with almost a half century later. They came from two distinct groups. One bunch was from my own class, the Stone Row crew, and included the aforementioned vipers from the D.C. area, a brilliant and funny black philosophy major from Harlem and a couple of wry dudes from a prep school in Pennsylvania. The other bunch was from the class of '68. These guys seemed more mature and tended to be more academically inclined. In fact, most had arrived at Bard with some already developed skills. Delmore could speak Chinese. Bexley, a composer, taught me proper musical notation, and Jonas won top prize for his senior thesis on Borges. Actually, it always seemed to me that the class of '68 was the last bunch of kids not seriously despoiled in their youth by television (with its insidious brainworm commercials) and drugs. Chances were they'd spent their first years of life without a TV and had to use their imagination to entertain themselves. Perhaps they'd even played with some non-corporate-developed toys and read a few books. Sans malls, they hung out at candy stores and had milk delivered by the milkman and the doctor came to their bedrooms when they were ill. Since then, TV and the malls and the drugs have annually compounded the Big Stupid we live with now.

That said, all these guys were now smoking enormous quantities of weed, which had just begun to be co-opted by the middle class. I smoked a fair amount myself until a series of anxiety attacks scared me off in the winter of 1967. For a while I thought the attacks had been triggered by the DMT my friends and I smoked during the big blizzard of that year. Dimethyltryptamine was the hallucinogen that Timothy Leary called the "businessman's trip" because of its intensity and brief duration. The intrepid Bard sophomore would load a pipe with a couple of parsley leaves that had been soaked with the stuff, take a toke and, just as it hit, run out into the stormy night. You'd go from zero to a peak acid-strength high in a nanosecond. The snow that was billowing across the campus was revealed as an army of tiny angels, and you wondered why you hadn't noticed that the college buildings huffed and puffed as if they were in a

Betty Boop cartoon from the thirties. Fifteen minutes later, everything looked normal except for a warm, lingering glow. Back to the dorm for another hit . . .

Mystic note: In the summer of 1965, a month before that first drive up to Bard, I'd already had my introduction to Oblivion. My friend Pete had gone off to Brandeis the year before and brought back a small cache of sugar cubes laced with five hundred micrograms of lysergic acid diethylamide, still perfectly legal at the time, and a book called *The Psychedelic Experience* by a trio of Harvard professors, including the notorious Dr. Leary before he went totally bat-shit loony. Inspired by a reference by Aldous Huxley in *The Doors of Perception*, the book was based on the Bardo Thodol (aka the Tibetan Book of the Dead), a Buddhist manual for the rebirth of the soul just as it leaves the body. Leary and his colleagues conceived their version as a road map for the serious tripper looking to achieve perfect ego death. (We're talking East Coast style here. Way out west, Ken Kesey was already using acid to clear the palate at beer parties.)

The thing about Leary's early method was, it had some nice features. Your guide, who remained drugless, assumed a role not unlike that of an empathic therapist. He arranged to have the session in a safe, agreeable environment and stayed with you through the whole experience, occasionally reading suggestive passages from the book that actually seemed, well, important at each successive stage of the journey.

On a beautiful Sunday, I dropped the acid at Pete's house. His family was a real anomaly in Kendall Park, the soul-strangling housing development our families were both living in at the time. His mother and father were classically trained actors who appeared at nearby McCarter Theatre in Princeton. His dad taught history at Rutgers as a day gig, and the walls of their living room were lined floor to ceiling with fat books and classical records. His mom, who knew what we were up to, kept buzzing around the kitchen, cutting flowers and slicing oranges in half—that sort of stuff.

And what did Donald learn? Well, LSD trips are famously impossible to describe, and impossibly boring to hear about as well. Let's just say that Dr. Leary's method was a resounding success. Afterwards, cruising at twilight through the carefully graded streets of Kendall Park in my beat-up '55 Ford Galaxy, I understood for the first time that all was as it should be, that the future was blazing with promise and that, despite all the jeers, Garden State might be a swell name for New Jersey after all.

Sometime during my sophomore year, I started playing with several student bands. There was a Chicago-type blues band, a noisy free jazz group and a sort of satirical pop group I'd put together to play the stuff I'd been writing. I decided to switch my major to music. I understood that, as was the case in most colleges at the time, the music department was governed by an unswerving faith in the cult of the academic avant-garde, which is to say postwar serial composition and its contemporary champions: Berio, Stockhausen, Cage, Boulez, et al. Jazz, then in the age of Miles Davis and John Coltrane, Charles Mingus and George Russell, and more than thirty years after Ellington, was still not considered a legitimate course of study, and it was inconceivable to think of popular music as anything but disposable trash. My guess is that, by the sixties, this policy had less to do with racism or social class than with the fact that these reactionary musics were—dare I say it?—tonal. Nevertheless, I figured I'd give it a go.

One afternoon in 1967, I walked over to the Red Balloon, a crummy little shack in the woods that served as an on-campus music club. As I approached, I could hear someone playing some electric blues guitar inside, just messing around. But this wasn't the trebly, surfadelic, white-guy sound I was used to hearing from other student guitarists. This fellow had an authentic blues touch and feel, and a convincing vibrato. His amp was tweaked to produce a fat, mellow sound, and turned up loud enough to generate a healthy Albert King–like sustain. Inside, playing a cranberry red Epiphone guitar, was a severe-looking bespectacled kid who would turn out to be my partner and bandmate for the next forty years.

Walter Becker and I had many interests in common: jazz, blues, all sorts of popular music, Nabokov and the writers of what was then called the "black humor" school, science fiction and so on. Walter shared an enormous room in Ward Manor with a dandyish wag by the name of Randall. Randall didn't seem to mind when Walter carted in two humongous Altec monitor speakers through which we blasted, for both pleasure and as a matter of professional interest, some of the great music of the time. We had very similar taste, which ran from Miles Davis to the Mothers of Invention, whom we had both seen during their infamous run at the Garrick Theater on Bleecker Street. Walter hipped me to inspiring stuff both old (Howlin' Wolf) and new (Laura Nyro) for the first time.

We started writing music and lyrics together, mostly on an

upright piano in a small sitting room in the lobby of the Manor. One of us would come up with some clowny idea and we'd bounce it around until we were so convulsed with laughter that we'd have to quit. For whatever reason, the combination of the funky grooves, the jazz chords and the sensibility of the lyrics, which seemed to fall somewhere between Tom Lehrer and *Pale Fire*, really cracked us up. Of course, at that point, what we were doing was pretty crude compared to some of our later efforts, but it was never less than fun.

We also played a few pickup gigs. One was for a student art show opening at the Procter Art Center. I had borrowed a Fender Rhodes keyboard from a big blond named Dinah. After pounding on the thing for a couple of tunes, the heavy instrument slipped off the table it was sitting on and crashed to the floor. Mortified and fearful of facing Dinah's wrath, I walked out of the place, leaving Walter to finish the set on his own. Unbeknownst to me, he had prepared for the performance by ingesting a powerful psychedelic and had to face the crowd in a state of total ganglial exposure. Sorry, W.B. And sorry, Dinah.

There was a lot of trouble back then with tripping musicians. Another time, we were hooked along with a drummer, Ike, to play an NAACP benefit at the Beekman Arms, an old hotel in Rhinebeck, just across the Hudson. In this case, it was the drummer who'd thought LSD would enhance his performance. For an hour or so, Walter and I struggled to lock in with Ike, who was sounding like Elvin Jones, literally, on acid. For the '67 Ward Manor Halloween party, we assembled a dance band that included our classmate Chevy Chase on drums. Chevy looked like a frat boy who'd wandered onto the wrong campus, but he was professional, talented and compulsively funny. He kept excellent time and, at least that night, didn't embarrass us by taking off his clothes or doing any of his Jerry Lewis bits. On the other hand, I, in a misguided attempt to effect holiday cheer, had stapled a string of large black faux-feathers to my long thrift shop overcoat. I ended up looking like an accident involving a giant crow and an electric fan. No matter—half the crowd was tripping anyway.

Walter dropped out at the end of the academic year in 1968. I began to lose interest in school. Missing the input of an actual jazz instructor, I started skipping classes, and despite the support I got from Jake "The Rake" Druckman, I was finally tossed out of the music department. I switched back to English, arranged my classes so they were all bunched together on Thursday and Friday, and moved to Brooklyn with Walter and my girlfriend, Dorothy White. We found two apartments in Park Slope, which had yet to become the Hipster Heaven that was to be. Back then, it was still Archie Bunker Heaven. It was the sort of neighborhood where shoulder-length hair could provoke comments like "Are you a boy or a girl?" and "Go back to the Village!" We persevered, and began our two-pronged assault on the music business: we began peddling pop tunes on Tin Pan Alley in midtown Manhattan and, at the same time, searched for players who might fit into the group we wanted to use as a vehicle for our prime stuff, the stuff we thought of as "the dynamite." But that's another story.

In May of '69, I was up at Bard for the weekend, working on the last draft of my senior thesis in an off-campus house I had rented with a couple of other students. At four in the morning,

the house and several men's dorms on campus were raided by
deputies of the local sheriff's department, along with some state
cops, under the aegis of the Dutchess County DA's office. Led
by soon-to-be Watergate burglar G. Gordon Liddy, then running for assistant DA, they were looking for any trace of marijuana, at that time still seriously illegal. Though I hadn't smoked
pot for quite a while, much less peddled any, they had a war-
rant for my arrest that included the testimony of a witness—in
fact our landlord, one Beau Coggins—who said I had sold him
drugs, "to wit, marijuana." Never mind the fact that I'd never
met the man (one of my roommates had rented the place and
paid the rent). By sunrise, some fifty kids had been paddy-
wagoned over to the Duchess County jail and locked in a cell
block, including me, Walter and Dorothy, who were both visiting. The guys were shorn of their long, treasured locks by a
trustee barber. After a day or so, the college bailed out all the
students, including former student Walter. They refused to do
the same for Dorothy, a nonstudent.

I called my father, then living in Ohio, who arranged bail for
Dorothy and then flew in so we could consult with the school's
attorney, Peter Maroulis. (In 1972, when that toxic little weasel
Liddy got popped for masterminding the Watergate break-in,
Maroulis was the guy he'd call.) A month later, our cases having
already been dismissed, I sat on a bench with Dorothy, my father
and Maroulis, watching the graduation of the class of '69. Because
the college had refused to bail out Dorothy, and because they'd let
the sheriff's office place an undercover spy with the building and
grounds department—he had been disguised as a janitor—I'd
decided to boycott the ceremony. Yeah, good times . . .

With the Dukes of September ▬▬▬

In December 1980, I was living three blocks away from the Dakota, watching Monday Night Football, *when Howard Cosell announced that John Lennon had been shot in the back. I walked over and watched as a huge crowd of sobbing New Yorkers gathered at Seventy-second Street and Central Park West. This pretty much set the tone of the decade to come. After delivering my album* The Nightfly *to Warner Brothers, I came apart like a cheap suit. The panic attacks I used to get as a kid returned, only now accompanied by morbid thoughts and paranoia, big-time. I could hardly get through the day, much less write music. I started seeing a shrink and gobbling antidepressants.*

Fast-forward to 1988. (Please!) I was feeling a lot better. A friend of mine, Libby Titus, was producing a series of what she called her "horrible little evenings" of music and comedy at restaurants around Manhattan. To make a long story short, we started collaborating; the project turned into the New York Rock and Soul Revue, which toured nationally for two years; and then we got married. Mike McDonald and Boz Scaggs were in the lineup of the 1993 tour. In 2010, we revived the concept as the Dukes of September Rhythm Revue. During the 2012 summer tour, I started keeping the journal that follows.

JUNE 19, 2012

This hotel, a Four Seasons on a highway in St. Louis, seems to be adjoined in some way to a casino and theater. Outside my seventeenth-floor window I can see an electric sign advertising future attractions down the way. An enormous picture of Eddie Griffin, the comedian, is followed by one of Tracy Morgan, and then Margaret Cho. There's also a video pushing a "mixed martial arts" event. Every minute or so in the rotation, there's a shot of a competitor slamming another man's red, swollen face down onto the mat with his elbow. This is followed by a picture of some well-shredded, half-naked Chippendale lads in a living room setting, relaxing on leather couches or on a plush carpet, recounting, I imagine, wild anecdotes about the previous night's performance.

I'm in town with this band, the Dukes of September Rhythm Revue, which is Michael McDonald, Boz Scaggs and me performing a program of moldy old R&B and soul tunes that we like, with some of our own hits thrown in to keep the TV Babies happy. The other players are mostly guys and gals I play with in the Steely Dan band, the group I started with my partner, Walter, which is off the road this year. The Dukes' first gig of the summer is on June 20, but we got here a couple of days early to do some tech rehearsals and clean up some loose ends at the Fox Theater, where the gig's going to be.

Aside from the rehearsals, I never leave the hotel room. Mainly, I've been lying in bed and thinking about cigarettes. I quit a couple of months ago and I do feel better except that it's like I'm always waiting for some square-ass civilian to finish a boring dinner story so I can go outside and have a cigarette, and that the square-ass civilian is now me.

That's not really true, about thinking only about smoking. Actually, right now I have a lot to do. It's my job to rehearse the band and make sure the arrangements get done on time and so forth. Also, I've been worrying about the set list, wondering if the sequence of songs is suitably dramatic and if the mix of our hits—McDonald's, Boz's, Steely Dan songs, my solo stuff—and cover tunes, many of which are probably unfamiliar to a lot of the TV Babies, is correct. Plus, although the three of us grew up with this mostly black music and feel pretty comfortable with it, I'm always feeling defensive and trying to minimize any perceived minstrelsy about the project. The fact that we've got two African American musicians, bassist Freddie Washington and singer Catherine Russell, doesn't really ease my mind in this regard, since the three principals are all white singers who have been heavily influenced by black style.

Food is primarily room service, which always involves an awkward phone call with a poor fucker who's been programmed to respond to everything you say with a perky "Absolutely!" and who's sworn to repeat your order to you, no matter how simple. Then there's the dance with the waiter, who's determined to get that cart in the door without your holding it open, and who also says "Absolutely!" a lot. For some years, it's been my feeling that the mechanized, brainless routines of many service people must have started with a cult-owned business, perhaps a restaurant chain operated by some sort of dead-eyed Christo-Fascists or Moonies or Orange People. It's that Sarah Palin talk: "Here's your prime rib for ya. Absolutely!"

At night, to get to sleep, I watch pay-per-view movies on the hotel system. The movies are so bad now that I usually pass out just after catching the first glimpse of the flesh-eating death-mist (or whatever), even before the archetypal hero has accepted the Campbellian Call to Adventure.

Once an insatiable reader, I don't read so much anymore. I'm now at the age—sixty-four—where so many sad things have happened that I'm too broken and anxious to read. I can still listen to music on the laptop, though, which is how I get to sleep after I've run out of pay-per-view movies.

JUNE 20

Back from the show. Basically fine, but we have to change the encore tunes. Mike singing Wilson Pickett's "In the Midnight Hour," which would have been a sure thing forty years ago, was, as Mike himself said afterwards, a death march. The TV Babies have never heard it, or could not care less. Or maybe it was just too on the nose.

Our next stop is Aspen, Colorado.

By the way, I'm not posting this journal on the Internet. Why should I let you lazy, spoiled TV Babies read it for nothing in the same way you download all those songs my partner and I sacrificed our entire youth to write and record, not to mention the miserable, friendless childhoods we endured that left us with lifelong feelings of shame and self-reproach we were forced to countervail with a fragile grandiosity and a need to constantly prove our self-worth—in short, with the sort of personality disorders that ultimately turned us into performing monkeys?

JUNE 22

We (which is to say me and Vince Corry, the tour accountant and my assistant this time around) arrived at the Denver airport late afternoon yesterday and picked up a proper tour bus and driver. Let me explain: Compared to a Steely Dan tour, the Dukes is more of a low-rent operation. With SD, the venues tend to be a little nicer and so are the travel conditions. While the band and crew schlep around on buses, Walter and I, whenever possible, "spoke" out of a major city where the nice hotels are, like LA or Chicago, and fly back and forth to the nearby gigs on a nifty chartered jet. It's pricey, but it saves wear and tear on the old guys. No jet for me this summer, though.

It was just three hours to Aspen, but on the way Vince got a call that the crew bus just ahead of us had caught fire and pulled over. Something to do with the brakes, the weight and the grade of the mountain highway.

Ten minutes later we picked up the stragglers, who were already drunk on Pasqual's Día de los Muertos tequila. Pasqual is an old friend of Walter's from Hawaii who's been working our tours the last few years. He's one of those indestructible roadies who goes back to the hippie days of glory with Bill Graham in San Francisco. He looks like a bandito, which he once actually sort of was. Lately he's been wearing a black hat that my wife, Libby, bought him last year.

It was good having the crew on the new bus for a while because, even when they're drunk, they walk around looking to see if anything needs to be fixed, test-flushing the toilets and asking me if I want my computer hooked up so I can play my iTunes through the bus's speaker system.

The Welkin Lodge in Aspen is advertised as "Perfect for pleasure-seekers. A high-style chill pad where beautiful people let loose . . . Come experience the secret behind the red velvet rope."

The truth of this statement is dependent on how you define "pleasure," "high style," "beautiful" and so on. For instance, you'd have to be able to extract "pleasure" from a "swim" in a tiny, paramecium-shaped pool surrounded by fake rock formations and filled with a tepid solution of semen and swamp water. At least, that's what it looked like. Nevertheless, needing some sort of exercise, I thrashed around for a few minutes, being careful not to let the water get near my mouth or nose. The only other person using the pool was a very large, Samoan-style man whose burly arms, and only his arms, were densely tattooed. He'd step in the "water" every fifteen minutes or so and lean against the side of the pool, cooling off, and then get out.

The pool is set in a kind of patio with tables and chairs where the "beautiful people" were chilling out and drinking special drinks. As I was getting out of the pool, a surfer-looking dude asked me if I was Donald Fagen. He said he was a big fan, and I gave my standard reply, which is "Oh, thanks. I appreciate it." Sometimes I'm tempted to affect a Southern accent and stutter a little on "I appreciate it," like Ray Charles. But I never do.

Aspen, the town, is an ordinary-looking but expensive shopping center where scary rich people are waited on by chunky, big-boned, blond hippie types. It has all the modem conveniences except for oxygen. If you look up, there are some nice mountains (I assume people ski down them in the winter). I didn't even see any pretty girls, although some of the girls I saw were wearing pretty shoes.

The show in the Benedict Music Tent was a lot better than the one in St. Louis, even though the sound onstage was atrocious, making it difficult to play. But that happens at least half the time.

Straight off the stage and on to the bus: ten hours to Vegas and a day off.

JUNE 23

I woke up on the bus, which was parked in the lot of the Hard Rock Hotel and Casino. ("If this house is a-rockin', don't bother knockin'.) Then Vince and I moved into rooms at the hotel.

I've been in this room before, or one just like it, with the large portrait of Kiss in the entrance hall and a framed black-and-white photo of the band cavorting with seven or eight groupies backstage. Though I'm not overly fastidious, all this tends to make me apprehensive about the sanitary condition of Vegas hotel rooms. I tiptoe around trying not to touch anything, wishing I'd brought a pair of surgical gloves.

If I wander around or eat in one of the restaurants at casino theater gigs, fans sometimes recognize me and want to talk. So that gives me an additional reason not to leave the room. No matter. With my bad attitude and all, a day off in Vegas is a season in hell. Once, in another lifetime, a gay friend, a philosophy professor, convinced me and my then girlfriend to accompany him on a Vegas weekend. He'd never been here, and he obviously saw it as a fabulous Disneyland of Camp, which I guess it is. We played the slots and he dragged us to a couple of shows. Ann-Margret's laser spectacular at Caesars Palace left me a bit cold. Seventies entertainer Lola Falana, who had to make do with the Aladdin's modest production values, was cute and kind of sad. Which is about as good as it ever gets here.

JUNE 25

This morning, the Dukes rolled into Humphreys Half Moon Inn and Suites, which is on an island in San Diego Bay. It has a little outdoor venue attached to it. After the show, just before we got back on the buses, I was approached by a woman who looked familiar, along with some family members. Back in the seventies, just before the tour for which we'd hired young Mike McDonald as a backup vocalist, we had these two perky chicks singing backup, Gloria and Jenny. Because they'd just come off a job where they worked in animal costumes at Disneyland, we called them Porky and Bucky. This woman was Jenny, that is, Bucky, who seemed to be doing just fine. Before the Disneyland gig, she used to float around suspended from a crane as Sally Field's stunt double on the TV show *The Flying Nun*. A typical CV in Hollywood. Neither of us knew what became of Porky. Last I remembered, she'd married an LA Dodger, Steve Yeager. But Bucky said they'd split up years ago. A nice moment: Bucky meets Carolyn Leonhart, the Bucky of the twenty-first century, or, actually, I think, the Porky.

JUNE 26

Nine hours on the bus to Santa Rosa in Sonoma County. I woke up at four a.m. and sat up front with Geoff, our British driver, as we cruised over the Bay Bridge into Marin. Nice country, if you're partial to that sort of thing.

We're spending the day off at the Hyatt Vineyard Creek

Hotel. There are certain hotels in pretty suburban areas like this one where you expect to see Rod Serling sitting in the lobby reading an out-of-date newspaper. As far as I can tell, there's no one staying here but me. No one at the pool, no one at the coffee shop. I know the whole band is supposed to be staying here, but where are they? Even Vince has disappeared. What's worse, I left my wallet in the room in San Diego. It was found, but it will take a day to FedEx and I forgot to ask Vince for money. So even if I wanted to cross the highway and take a look at that shopping center—I don't—I couldn't buy anything. I have no idea where the actual town of Santa Rosa is, but why bother to ask.

I've noticed that, on off days, some band members do their laundry—at least, the girls do. (In the seventies, I used to throw my underwear in the sink and pour in some Woolite.) Walt Weiskopf (sax and flute) and Freddie Washington (bass) play golf. Asking me to play golf would be like asking me to drive over to the town dump and separate all the wrongly placed bottles and cans from the regular garbage. That's how I think of it. So, again, I'm holed up in my room. I can't work on music on the road. It just doesn't happen. So I'm writing this.

I always associate Northern California with the late sixties, when I spent some time here. The hippie stuff was fun for about five minutes and then, by late '67, the barbarism had set in.

A typical story: A woman I know made the mistake of accepting the invitation of a famous "hippie" songwriter to spend the day on his houseboat in Mendocino, where he proceeded to beat the hell out of her and, for a time, kept her there at gunpoint. Luckily, she escaped and told her friend Sonny Barger, then president of the Oakland Hells Angels, about it.

Sonny sent a crew roaring upstate, where they worked the guy over and burned down his boat. In those days of love and peace, you'd hear that sort of stuff all the time.

JUNE 27

On the bus, rumbling toward LA. The Santa Rosa gig was at the Wells Fargo Center for the Arts, which used to be called something else. (Just about every place used to be called something else two years ago, and something else before that.) Also, I've noticed that the venues seem to be getting smaller every night. My manager, Irving Azoff, who, over the years, has acquired a piece of just about every valuable asset in the music business (or what's left of it), including the acts, the venues, the company you have to buy the tickets from and various other entities that just seem to spit back money at him, tells me that it's "because the Dukes ain't Steely Dan."

The thing is, lately, when I tour with Steely Dan, the venues also seem to be shrinking. Of course, I'm being disingenuous. Mike, Boz and I are pretty old now and so is most of our audience. Tonight, though, the crowd looked so geriatric I was tempted to start calling out bingo numbers. Nevertheless, by the end of the set they were all on their feet, albeit shakily, rocking out to Mike's performance of Buddy Miles's "Them Changes." So this, now, is what I do: assisted living.

JUNE 28

The show at the Gibson Amphitheatre in LA would be a big deal if we were a promising band of young lads, or even us, like, thirty or forty years ago, when we didn't have these idiotic white beards. Nevertheless, the house was decent and Fox News cameras were there, although that might be because Bill O'Reilly is a big fan of McDonald, I kid you not. There were a fair number of backstage guests, including two musical Bobs, Bob Neuwirth and Bob Thiele Jr.; Connie Stevens, who used to play Cricket on *Hawaiian Eye* in the fifties (hey, she's a fan); James Gadson, an all-star R&B drummer I've worked with; jazz writer Devon Wendell, who used to be an intern at River Sound, my erstwhile recording studio in New York; and my cousin Alan Rosenberg, an actor, and his ex-wife, Marg Helgenberger, also an actor, who's famous from TV and very good looking and always provokes a stir backstage.

Also my manager Irving and a "friend," Matty. Irving, who's leprechaun-sized, often travels with one of these "friends"— really bodyguards—who all look like they were Navy Seals or mob enforcers or some combination of both. I guess he's afraid of being kidnapped and held for ransom or maybe just mugged in a parking lot, though I can't imagine him not being able to talk his way out of a sticky situation.

JUNE 29

Waking up in the overchilled back bedroom of the bus with the thick shades locked down is like waking up in a dark, dusty shoe box on a shelf in the basement of a Florsheim shoe store in, say, Utica, New York, in 1953. Staggering up to the front, I saw that we were parked across the street from the Miramar Hotel in bright, downtown San Jose. A day off here. Oh. Great.

Yesterday I sent a gripe e-mail to Irving about the insane bus routing, that is, the boomeranging from Northern to

Southern California and back again, which, aside from wasting diesel fuel, is hard on drivers, musicians and the crew. Now, I know I should have caught this earlier myself, and I also know that Irving is semiretired and really doesn't concern himself with this stuff anymore. Nevertheless, I needed to break someone's nuts about it.

It was interesting. Irv's first reaction was to accept responsibility but to claim that the available dates in the venues we wanted necessitated the crazy routing. Then, after thinking about it a minute, he decided to blame it all on McDonald's and Boz's managers, Jack and Joel. Then he tried to make Vince the scapegoat, but Vince had already told me he'd brought the matter up weeks ago but had received no response.

Finally Irv demanded an explanation from Marc Robbins, who works for him. Marc seemed to think the problem was that the Dukes had opted for buses instead of chartering a jet. Of course, we had previously been warned that this would've been too expensive. I finally told these backpedaling desperados to knock it off and just remember not to screw it up again. Christ.

Again, I tried to swim a bit in the hotel pool. The Miramar has one outdoors in the back. The trick is to get there early, when it's relatively empty, which I did. An hour later, it was teeming with screeching children, plump moms and the big, bullet-headed, tattooed family men you now see all across the country. Are they ex-military? Domesticated bikers? Professional wrestlers? I don't know.

I've started to exhibit early symptoms of Acute Tour Disorder (see Appendix). One is sleep trouble, although, at the Miramar, I think it's because the sheets and pillowcases smell like soy sauce, a common occurrence in hotels. Is it because they use some particular noxious detergent? Or is it what everyone's thinking, that the launderers are Chinese people who eat while they're working and allow certain food elements to mix with the cleaning elements? Or would it seem totally paranoid to imagine that certain disgruntled, vengeful workers might actually pour their bottles of soy sauce into the washing machines or dryers?

I finally manage to get to sleep by listening to an old Verve album I have on my computer, "Getz Meets Mulligan in Hi-Fi." These two white jazz virtuosos, both acolytes of Lester Young, both ex-junkies and heavy drinkers, and both, according to musicians' lore, megalomaniacal dicks, played like angels, and never more so than on this album. I've been listening to it for a half century, and it always seems fresh and beautiful.

JUNE 30

Speaking of megalomaniacal dicks—I was about to comment on how it's impossible to be a working artist without being somewhat of a megalomaniacal dick, but I need to think about that more.

JULY 1

Last night's show in San Jose was the best so far, with the crowd really into it and dancing and screaming. For one thing, it was Saturday night, which, for any number of reasons, disinhibits the crowd. Also the crowd was mostly around the right age, and not too many TV Babies.

Incidentally, by "TV Babies" I mean people who were born

after, say, 1960, when television truly became the robot care-taker of American children and therefore the principal archi-tect of their souls. I've actually borrowed the term from the film *Drugstore Cowboy*, in which Matt Dillon, playing a drug addict and dealer, uses it to refer to a younger generation of particularly stupid and vicious dealers who seem to have no souls at all.

The Paramount Theatre in Oakland is one of those old art deco movie palaces from the thirties. It's pretty gorgeous in that kitschy sort of way. By the sixties, many of these theaters served as rock venues. Although they can be fun to play in, they have their drawbacks. Many of them still have poor ventilation. The dressing rooms are often old, tiny and ill equipped; same with the bathrooms.

One of the oddest things is the security personnel. There's always "security" backstage, men and women who sit in Sam-sonite folding chairs on the stairwells and on the landings who, theoretically, make sure that no one is wandering around back-stage without a pass. I'm not talking about the Secret Service here. In the old theaters, for this sedentary, unskilled job, they often hire people who have been associated with the building for, like, forever, and that sometimes means old show people or what Levon Helm used to call "rounders"—assorted wannabes and crazies, folks who just like to hang around with perform-ers. I like most of them; they usually turn out to be pretty nice. But when you're kind of wasted after a long bus ride, it can still be a shock to climb the stairs to your dressing room and have to walk past a woman sitting on the landing in a flannel bathrobe and flip-flops with a face that looks like the tragic result of a fire in a wax museum, wearing a wig-hat made of blue yarn. In a certain, vulnerable frame of mind, I can be quite squeamish about such things. And yet, I suppose she's there to protect me from people who are even crazier than she is.

JULY 1

Back to the artist as a megalomaniacal dick: Just like in the civilian population, a nasty, rude fucker is nasty and rude because they're scared of what you think of them. It's a defense. Sometimes, the same stuff that made them so scared has also contributed to their creative nature, though I've found that the most unpleasant ones are usually mediocre artists as well. This is because real art—I'm generalizing here—requires a certain level of empathy.

Of course, an artist has to maintain control. This means making sure conditions are right, which includes being unsentimental about tossing people who aren't doing their job or who reveal themselves to be psychos or whatever. But even firing folks can be done with kindness.

In his autobiography, Charles Mingus remembered the graceful way Duke Ellington canned him after he got into a fight with the trombonist Juan Tizol:

> "Now Charles," he says, looking amused, putting Cartier links into the cuffs of his beautiful handmade shirt, "you could have forewarned me . . . For a moment I was hopeful you'd decided to sit down and play but instead you slashed Juan's chair in two with a fire axe! Really, Charles, that's

destructive. Everyone knows Juan has a knife but nobody ever took it seriously—he likes to pull it out and show it to people, you understand. So I'm afraid, Charles—I've never had to fire anybody—you'll have to quit my band. I don't need any new problems. Juan's an old problem. I can cope with that, but you seem to have a whole new bag of tricks."

Duke was a true artist.

Then again—just every once in a while, no matter how bad it makes you feel—there's no option but to come down on some ungrateful, arrogant, persistent little punk like you're Godzilla on angel dust.

JULY 2

There was something intensely creepy about the Canary Hotel in downtown Santa Barbara, so I moved to where the band is staying, out by the beach, Fess Parker's DoubleTree Resort. All us boomers know that Fess played Davy Crockett on TV in the fifties and started a national craze for coonskin caps.

Once in my room, I couldn't seem to get online. When I called the front desk, they told me that, in the space labeled "Promotional Code," I had to type in the password RAY-THEON2012. The girl at the desk had obviously mistaken me for a corporate conventioneer or some such thing. Then I remembered that Raytheon makes a lot of cool, deadly stuff, like, for instance, Stinger missiles and torpedoes and cruise missiles and even a giant laser cannon that, so far, the military's been too scared to actually use. Maybe, with this password, I could go home with a little ray gun in a goodie basket or something. Seriously: I wonder if the lingering image of Fess Parker with that coonskin cap, that symbol of an innocent yet strong America, had something to do with the choice of the DoubleTree for a Raytheon corporate powwow.

Tonight Pasqual took me and a couple of other band members to a funky little Mexican restaurant. Afterwards, waiting for a cab, we stood around staring at a green 1964 Porsche convertible parked outside.

It's late. I woke up and heard an ominous noise in the hall, several times now. It sounds like an amplified exhalation, or some steam escaping from a locomotive, followed by a double thump or knock. Now I've imagined there's a terrible Hound from Hell running loose in the hotel. Maybe it was that Mexican food. I'd give my right arm for a cigarette. I'm turning on all the lights.

JULY 3

Eleven a.m. I'm awake. Horrible dreams. I realize I've been sleeping on the white square thing that's on the Apple AC cord that's hot as a charcoal briquette.

I'm fairly certain that I'm now suffering from some of the anxiety symptoms on the ATD list, the psychological stuff: the insomnia, a little paranoia, maybe a touch of mania. I just ventured out to find some breakfast and check out the pool. The vast lobby had several dining areas with many tables, couches, nooks and so on, but only one couple was seated and they seemed to be having cocktails. Fighting a nameless terror, I asked a doorman how to get to the pool and he directed me outside, where I followed a path that led through an underpass to a medium-sized one already cluttered with kids. I was still hungry but the poolside stand seemed to be selling only burgers and hot dogs. I ended up making my way through the winding, expressionist hallways back to my room, settling for a warm Snickers bar and a Sprite. I'm just going to wait for Vince to call and tell me what to do next.

JULY 4

I'm feeling better this morning, having slept many hours on the bus during the eleven-hour trip to—where?—the Plaza Inn and Suites in Ashland, Oregon, a quaint sort of place, a college town and the home of the Oregon Shakespeare Festival. When I got off the bus, stiff and bleary eyed, there was a July Fourth parade in progress, featuring sorrowfully overweight teenage girls holding tiny flags. I just heard the loud *crooosh* of a fighter jet streaking overhead.

Geoff went off immediately to sleep. By the way, McDonald and Boz also have their own buses. The band, twelve players in all, is split between two buses. The crew also has a bus, plus there are the two trucks that carry the sound and lighting gear.

When Steely Dan started touring again in the early nineties, the band divided naturally into two distinct social groups, which gave the two buses their names: the Soul Bus and the Horn Bus. The current Soul Bus is mostly the rhythm section, including Freddie, guitarist Jon Herington, keyboard man Jim Beard and Catherine. It's more of a party bus sort of situation. The Horn Bus, which I call the Nerd Bus, is dominated by the more neurasthenic, introspective types—you know, the Jewish people: trumpeter Michael Leonhart and his sister Carolyn, and reed men Walt Weiskopf and Jay Collins. I've ridden both buses on short runs and they're both fun. Shannon, the drummer, and an old pal of McDonald's, usually rides with Mike.

Predictably, the Soul Bus is good for kidding around, funky playlists, singing, a really nice hang. Freddie watches old movies on TCM. The Horn Bus is a little quieter. They also watch films, try to decimate each other at Scrabble and there are a couple of wickedly funny people. Horn players talk about their mouthpieces and reeds *a lot*. As far as I can tell, there's about the same amount of (generally moderate) alcohol consumption on both buses. You couldn't ask for a mellower bunch of cats and kitties. And they're all mighty road warriors, not puny malcontents like myself.

As I've mentioned, when Steely Dan is touring, Walter and I stay in nice hotels. The band usually stays in somewhat cruddier hotels, and the crew, God bless 'em—I don't know where they stay. On the Dukes tour, though, I'm often with the band on the cruddy level, though not tonight in Ashland, where Vince and I are in our own cruddy hotel.

Okay, not cruddy—sort of charming, really, but someone did only perfunctory research: no room service at the Plaza Inn. After threading our way through the intense holiday crowd scene on the streets of Ashland (bands, food concessions, etc.), Vince and I found a sort of fern bar that was open for lunch. Passing the town square, we were surprised to see an operational "lithia fountain" spewing out water from an underground spring that's apparently rich in lithium salts. Being aware of the salubrious effect of pharmaceutical lithium on manic-depressives, I considered taking a sip, but was finally put off by sanitation concerns. Oh, well.

In the evening, having zero interest in the town fireworks display, Vince and I saw a film at the cute little movie theater, Wes Anderson's *Moonrise Kingdom*, which was intelligent and carefully made, as his films always are. Walter and I once had a bizarre interaction with Anderson's fans over the Internet, which started when we posted a couple of humorous letters (we thought) on the Steely Dan website.

I think one of the reasons we're intrigued by Anderson is that he seems to be fixated on the sort of geekish, early-sixties adolescent experience that he's too young to have had but that Walter and I actually lived through. And yet he nails the mood precisely, using comic exaggeration and fantasy to do the job. Although it was no picnic, it's too bad everyone's coming-of-age can't take place in the early sixties. Seeing the scouts in *Moonrise Kingdom*, I was reminded of my own experience at Boy Scout camp. I remember spending a lot of time in my tent worrying over a huge pot of boiling water in which I was trying to brew just the right blend of herbal tea, mostly wintergreen picked in the forest, following some recipe in the Scout handbook.

JULY 5

Speaking of tea, I guess some Snapple leaked onto my MacBook Pro keyboard so that now some keys are sticky and make a disturbing sucking noise. Plus, we're at an uncomfortable gig in Medford, Oregon. Backstage, there's heinously bad feng shui or whatever you call it, cramped dressing rooms (the girls' room is in the kitchen), two little bathrooms for, like, fifty backstage people. Can't wait to crash out of here.

JULY 6

I'm finally back in a civilized hotel, the Four Seasons on Elliott Bay in Seattle, though only for a few hours. Just outside, I see they now have one of those giant Ferris wheels like in Paris and London. They have a serious spa here and there's just time enough to get a massage.

I drew a girl—let's call her Naomi—who was young and pretty, which is always nice. But she looked a little scrawny for the job.

Working on the backs of my calves with some minty oil, she asked me if I wanted her to go deeper, so I said sure, a little bit. Suddenly Naomi from Seattle turned into Rosa Klebb, the SMERSH interrogator from the James Bond series. I couldn't believe the force with which she was driving her knobby little knuckles into my petrified muscles and tendons. It was excruciating, but I have this stupid thing—like, no son of Staff Sergeant Joseph Fagen, veteran of the Big One, is going to whine about a little pain in front of some strange girl. Finally, all greased up and smelling like a Twizzler, I limped into the elevator in my bathrobe, crab-walked back to my room and started to pack for the gig.

JULY 7

Okay, that's it. Not even three weeks out and I'm starting to crumble. I feel crazy. It's time to assess my condition and make some recommendations.

Also, I feel like I was beaten by bullies while I was asleep. Maybe that massage. Singing too hard, I think I blew a gasket. I can feel it in my throat. The bones in my fingers are throbbing from pounding the keys like a baboon. I woke up in Vancouver, BC, but I can't exactly remember where we played last night. Oh—a winery gig a couple of hours from here. Tonight we play in a theater in town. That will make three shows in three days, not nice for elderly singers. There are a couple of three-day runs on this tour, which I mostly avoid with Steely Dan. But as Irving says, "This tour ain't Steely Dan." Luckily, with the Dukes, I'm singing only a third of the time.

It's true that at about this point in every tour, the nice little plans and resolutions I made previously become irrelevant. Swimming? Pools are grungy or freezing or crowded or there's just not enough time. Treadmill in the hotel gym? Go fuck yourself—I'm too wasted to exercise. Someone suggested, well, why don't I try bicycling? You mean, call the concierge, inquire about rentals, roll around unfamiliar streets while cars and trucks are trying to kill me? I can't even get the hell out of bed. I know, I'm in a comfortable room in another Four Seasons Hotel with a view of the harbor. So fucking what? I've been spoiled over the years and, anyway, it doesn't matter where you are when your body hurts and you're depressed and angry. Right now, I'm too mentally ill to even order breakfast. Until I cool out, I dread any contact with another human being. Back in the day, as the kids say, my wife used to accompany me on tour, at least part of the time, so it was easier. But she's had enough of that now and she's busy at home.

Some might say, But wait—don't you have a personal

assistant who can make all this easier for you? I once had a pretty good one on a Steely Dan tour. The answer is no: times are tough, too expensive. I guess I could force myself to call Vince and have him check out the pool or call the concierge or call room service. But, though Vince is great, his main gig is tour accountant, and the "Donald's tour manager" thing is just because we need to economize. Like, it's obvious that Vince has a thing about carrying other people's luggage. To Vince, my suitcase might as well be an isotope of Cesium 137. Fair enough, but he's just not cut out to be a personal assistant. Plus, I've never been comfortable ordering people to do little stuff like that. On the road, Madonna and Mick Jagger have personal assistants, trainers, vegan chefs and, I don't know, ass buffers who they can order around and abuse. But this isn't that sort of thing.

Here's the deal: If I were just the piano player, it would be fine. My mother was a great natural singer, but I fell into the job by accident—I have to work like a dog just to get it out. And loud electric music is a whole other thing: you're fighting the amps, the delayed blowback off the walls, the screaming monitors (I've tried those in-ear monitors you see singers use on TV: I felt way too alienated from my labor). Then there's the pressure of being the front man and the trauma of facing the crowd. Three weeks out, you start to pay the price. Don't get me wrong, I love the work, but my sixty-four-year-old body and brain are starting to fail.

You may be wondering, What's the problem, dude? Sure, travel's tough on an old guy, it's a gnarly gig, but, really, why are you so beat up? Well, here's what it's about, and this isn't in the ATD description: For a lot of performing artists, every night in front of an audience, no matter how exhilarating, is a bit of a ritual slaying. Without necessarily letting it show, you use every last bit of your marrow, every last atom of your energy in an attempt to satisfy the hungry crowd. On some level, you're trying to extinguish yourself. Because, corny and Red Shoes-y as it may seem, that's what you are, and they need it. And it's exhausting.

The Orpheum in Vancouver is home to the Vancouver Symphony Orchestra. For all I know, the orchestra sounds spectacular in this place. But, as is the case with many old symphony halls, when you're playing electric music at pretty high volume, you might as well be playing in an airplane hangar. If there's a sonic hell, the entrance is somewhere on the stage of the Orpheum in Vancouver. *Entre nous*, I suspect they built these places hoping the monstrous reverberation off every surface would disguise how rotten the orchestras actually were.

Dazed with fatigue, I barely made it though the sound check. Then I remembered that, in Canada, it's possible to get a tablet over the counter containing aspirin or Tylenol, caffeine and—here's the good part—eight milligrams of codeine. It's marketed as 222 or AC&C. I mean, William Burroughs definitely couldn't be bothered, but, if you take four of them, it's almost as good as taking a Tylenol 3 with codeine, I think. It might just hit the spot. So I had Vince send a runner out to score a few bottles (not Pasqual; they stopped him at the border because of some unresolved issues). By showtime, I was feeling a little better.

In Bill Bradley's book *Life on the Run,* about playing for the Knicks in the seventies, there's a description of going back to the motel after another punishing game (he was a small forward, always getting beat up, sometimes by Wilt Chamberlain, no less) and collapsing into a bathtub filled with ice water. Oh, brother. Imagine that.

It's no wonder so many traveling performers end up in rehab or worse. It's easy to see how it happens. They want to be alert and vibrant so that the audience won't think badly of them, won't punish them for not being as talented or magnetic as you thought they were. So that your crush won't suddenly end. I know, it's pathetic.

JULY 8

The crowd at the Orpheum was the oldest yet. They must have bused in people from nursing homes. There were people on slabs, decomposing, people in mummy cases.

Also, they were Canadian, by which I mean to imply that they've inherited their culture from Britain. As is the case in Japan, another island nation where folks are all squeezed together in a small space, Brits, by necessity, had to evolve a system of rigorous interpersonal courtesy so that they wouldn't tear each other apart. Fine, except that there are side effects: the more civilization, the more repression. So, unlike typical American audiences presented with an irresistible groove, Canadians (at least when they're sober) just sit motionless for two hours, fighting every impulse to nod, tap a foot, say hooray or move any part of their bodies. That is, until the big finish of the show, when, as their superegos are no longer able to contain the furious directive of the lower brain, they rise to their feet and, at last, explode with bestial cries and applause. Of course, when islanders drink, it's a different story. As Freud liked to say, the superego is soluble in alcohol.

JULY 9

Vince and I flew into Denver last night (again, the yo-yo routing). Another Four Seasons Hotel, except that instead of a Ferris wheel, I can see a roller coaster out the window and imagine the people screaming. The gig at the Paramount's not until tomorrow, so it's a day off.

I really don't know a lot about Denver, except that, like Aspen, the altitude makes it harder to sleep, breathe and think. The place still has that boomtown vibe, maybe because it's so flat, like a board game. Two of the most famous con men of all time, Lou Blonger and Soapy Smith, operated out of Denver. Neal Cassady, Kerouac's pal, grew up here stealing cars.

When Steely Dan was playing here a few years ago, our opening act, organist Sam Yahel, was driving through a nasty snowstorm when he was stopped by the police for "weaving in the lane" or something like that. Mind you, he was driving on icy roads in a blizzard. A sweet, talented guy, Sam's got a beard and unruly hair and looks like he might very well be from Jew York City. So the cop makes him get out of the car, walk in a straight line, count backward, all that stuff, and finally says, "I can't catch ya, but I know yer on sumpin' by just lookin' in your eyes." He kept Sam, his drummer and his bass player over an hour, but finally had to let them go. They just made the gig on time. Again, this didn't happen in 1969. This was 2009. The point being, if y'all have to be in Denver, you best mind yer p's and q's. But that might not be enough.

JULY 10

I force myself to take the elevator to the third-floor rooftop pool. Very few people around in the early afternoon. A couple of rich wifey types and a block of obviously gay men. I later found out there was a large convention of choristers in town.

After a swim, I was tricked into ordering lunch by a trio of rather exotic, good-looking pool girls who had been carefully coached, or so it seemed, to be initially seductive and then abruptly aloof, like the femme fatale characters in hard-boiled novels. The way it worked was, they turn on the heat when they welcome you to the pool area and get you to look at the menu, behaving as if you were James Bond, using all sorts of lip-pursings and sly looks over the shoulder as they walk off with the drink tray, and so on. After being asked about the menu several times, I finally gave in and ordered something, though I wasn't particularly hungry. From then on, all three sirens either ignored me completely or, if they happened to catch my eye, looked at me as if I were a lump of shit. They seemed to be giving all their attention to the gay choristers. As I was leaving, tying my sneakers, gathering up my newspaper, the girls became suddenly alert, chased me down and made sure I signed the check. Then they stood in a line and watched me, now a broken, sorry creature, as I walked toward the elevator bank.

Back from the gig. I just sent this e-mail:

From: Donald Fagen
To: Irving Azoff
Subject: Jeez . . .
i can't believe the dumps we're playing—
the paramount in denver—
hot as hell—
no proper dressing rooms—
and here i am, as old as my cigar-chomping uncles when they
started dropping dead walking up grove street in passaic—
that's it: i'm leaping dimensions—
i'll see you on july 11, 2 pm, in the year 6004 at the corner of
higgs and unix in celestion city—
and bring some rye bread . . .
df

From: Irving Azoff
To: Donald Fagen
Subject: Jeez . . .
Donald. You need to do steely dan if you don't want to play
dumps. You guys as dukes have no profile, no record, no dvd,
don't play the tv press game. Unless you whore yourself out you
get to play dumps. Sorry. People don't give a shit about live shows
anymore unless you really work it.

From: Donald Fagen
To: Irving Azoff
Subject: Jeez . . .
see you in celestion city—
df

JULY 11

A lot of well-known bands play "privates," which is to say private affairs and parties, because the money is usually excellent. Often you're asked to "meet and greet" the organizers, pose for some photos with some guys and otherwise show how glad you are to be there.

The worst are corporate gigs where the band is hired to perform in front of several hundred or a hundred or even fifty suits at a convention or company party. They usually sit at tables, dinner theater–style, maybe with their wives or, just as often, hired escorts, and consume a lot of hard liquor. If they've hired a top band, it means they've had a good year and the leadership has invested in a real blowout, a wang dang doodle, although they never look as though they're having much fun. The hookers like to get up and dance.

Because these gigs are so depressing, I (and Walter, when out with SD) usually pass on the offers. First off, I have a hard time being around wealthy types and, as I'm a terrible actor, it's hard to fake it. Then there's the way rich people usually treat musicians. Aside from a couple of years playing in the rhythm section for the pop group Jay and the Americans in the early seventies, Walter and I never had a lot of experience as "the help use the back door" types. We just weren't in the same world as the players who did weddings and bar mitzvahs and such. Occasionally, we were talked into playing a studio date for an advertising agency or something like that. But we never had to participate in too many sessions that didn't involve our own music.

When our job as staff songwriters at ABC/Dunhill Records failed spectacularly, the boss, Jay Lasker, gave us a budget to record our own album, *Can't Buy a Thrill*, which hit big right out of the box. So, compared to the way most fledgling musicians and songwriters are treated, we were pretty spoiled. And anyway, talent aside, we were perceived as artists just by virtue of our wisenheimer personalities and transparent resentment of authority.

Now, the Dukes' gig at the Vilar Performing Arts Center in Beaver Creek, Colorado, this evening wasn't a private. But it felt like one. Maybe it was the altitude, but as soon as I got to the venue, I started to get my paranoiac-anarcho-surrealist freak on. It's a deluxe little theater built by the Vail Valley Foundation for the community. Beautiful lobby, comfortable seats, good sound system. And yet, the food that catering served the band and crew was god-awful, the worst on the tour so far (this happens quite often at privates, too). Plus, instead of a proper dining hall, or even a room set aside that's connected to the kitchen, they set up a few tables on the loading dock right off the wing, stage left.

By curtain time, I was ready for action by any means necessary. If these people could only see into the mind of the viperous Robespierre they had invited into their midst . . . (I think my expression might have worried a few of the band members, but, mostly, this radical fairy tale was just going on in my head.) Aside from throwing some withering glares at the stewed, swaying ski chicks in the second row and the fact that I kept messing up the song order, I got through the show okay. But by the time we got offstage, after enduring the not unenthusiastic but not quite authentic response from the tanned and strangely dissociated crowd, I had entered a kind of merciless fugue state. I imagined it was early morning and I could see the chunky, now hungover blond princesses and their defeated fathers standing in the rickety open carts, hands bound behind their backs, as they rolled up to the Place de la Révolution to be guillotined by the brawny, black-masked executioner.

JULY 13

Ah, waking up in Tulsa on a midsummer morning with a wicked sinus headache. I was too tired after the flight from Denver to deal with the thermostat, so there's a lot of dry, cold air flowing in from somewhere. Or maybe it's the altitude change. Let's see, where's that Canadian codeine? Also some Claritin, I think.

This room in the Hyatt is dang ugly, cowboy. Isn't there some design rule that says the floral pattern on the wallpaper can't be duplicated on the carpet? I feel like I'm living inside one of my aunt Lotty's doilies.

Eight forty a.m. central time now. I'm putting on the Stravinsky and going back to sleep.

JULY 14

Bastille Day. Apparently, our bus, traveling to Tulsa while we flew, broke down somewhere in Kansas. A part needs to be FedEx-ed from Canada to Wichita to get it moving again. So Vince and I are now glomming a ride to Dallas on McDonald's bus. Our bus should meet us there.

I feel a lot better now that we're at a normative altitude. I've had symptoms of altitude sickness in the past but, because I'm an idiot, I left those pills in NYC. I guess oxygen depletion in the brain can cause all sorts of psychological aberrations that are the same as the items on the ATD list, so there are too many variables working here to really know what's what. Moreover, I've had bizarre anxiety symptoms all my life, as a kid, as a teenager and in my thirties and early forties. After ten years of therapy and, bolstered by a powerful daily cocktail of psychotropic pharmaceuticals, I've been doing pretty well for some time now. Yeah, it must have been the altitude.

A Japanese promoter, the mighty Mr. Udo, wants the Dukes to do a few dates in October. If Irving can get the price up, I guess we'll go. It's not easy to finance an Asian excursion for a band of this size.

It's only for a week or so, which is fine, because Japan is rough for me. First of all, to a Westerner, it looks like an amusement park on Mars. You might as well be trying to find your way around the inside of a pinball machine. Plus, American musicians complain about the killer jet lag—the day-for-nighttime change—and the stress of communicating with a radically different culture. For someone like me, who freaks out in, like, Beaver Creek, you can imagine how unhinged I feel in Japan.

Again, it's the island nation problem, and again there are some parallels with British culture, though Japan is an extreme case. The intensely formal code of courtesy, especially when dealing with foreigners, causes a lot of misunderstanding. Here's a Japan story our guitarist likes to tell:

Late one night, Jon and a few other players walked into a restaurant and asked if they could still get something to eat. The waitress looked slightly upset but said, Oh yes, come in. Is there a table available? Oh yes, please sit here. Could we get some menus? The waitress, almost in tears, brought the menus. Can we order, please? She finally bowed her head and came out with it: Oh—so sorry, we closed.

There you have it: because there are apparently no words in the language that actually express the concept *no*, the promoters, the club employees, the drivers, even the sympathetic translators, are all forced into lying about almost everything. My wife, who, for various reasons, including one or two unreliable parents, is severely allergic to mendacity or any sort of equivocation, no matter how subtle, can never go there again. I guess I can endure it for a week for some easy green.

Okay, I'm back on my own bus, heading to Austin. It's all good. The show at the Verizon Theatre in Grand Prairie, a suburb of Dallas, was disappointing, especially since the venue's acoustics were so slick. The previous night in Tulsa had turned out to be a gas, a great crowd. Tonight, though, too many TV Babies out there. They mainly wanted to hear the hits they knew from when they were kids, or from their parents' vinyl collection, or classic radio. Those sleek, tipsy Dallas babes with the expensive dresses and coifs and earrings, you know they'd be real goers if they weren't with their spouses. One of them in the front row in a white dress would get up and dance for a minute with her eyes closed and her arms in the air and then, reined in by the hubby and the other couple she was with, would sit back down, defeated. Every night, there's always some chick out there who'll yell, "We love you, Michael," or "I love you, Boz," and once in a while I'll get one of those too. But usually, with me, because of the "musicians' musician" thing and various other disqualifiers, it'll be some poor dude yelling *"DONNNNALD"* in a crazy, tortured voice.

JULY 15

Okay, okay, I confess. I've had a few cigarettes, but only bumming them at the gigs and from Geoff the driver. Today, at Austin City Limits, I smoked a Newport on the terrace, watching dark clouds roll in over the street, the beginning of a storm. I called home and Libby checked her various devices to see if there was a tornado involved, but I guess not. This is the third of another three-show stretch. I'm falling asleep standing up.

The last time I played in Austin was in the early seventies at a legendary counterculture rock palace called the Armadillo World Headquarters. We were opening, I think, for a group called Rare Earth, a white group signed to Motown that became successful doing covers of Temptations tunes. They had a good singing drummer. It was a big, funky room filled with reefer smog, good clean fun. Now it's a parking lot or something. Today, on the private dining menu at the Four Seasons, you can order something called a "Hippie Salad."

JULY 16

After a show, if it's a longish drive to the next location, I'll sleep on the bus for a while. When we arrive, we move into the new hotel in the wee hours. While Vince gets the keys at the desk, I stand in the lobby, bleary eyed, watching the cleaners vacuum the rugs and wax the floors with those big chrome machines. This morning, when we stepped into the elevator, a young black guy was polishing the metal ornaments with a product called "Brite Boy."

Most of the time, McDonald and Scaggs save money on hotels by having the bus drive straight to the parking lot of the next gig—in other words, they never get off the bus. I've tried that a few times. It felt more like the lifestyle of an insect than a human.

JULY 17

Exhausting show in Houston. Outdoor gig with a rare air-conditioned stage, but the humidity was still crushing. The effect was that of an irritating polar draft in hell. The whole Oklahoma/Texas run has been a grind. Again, I'm starting to wilt. And the luxury hotel in, say, Houston isn't what you might expect. It's a depressed town right now, and the hotel is old and ailing, like me. I keep thinking of that Jim Thompson novel *A Swell-Looking Babe*, in which the young protagonist gets a job as a bellhop in an Oklahoma City hotel and is initiated into a shadowy world of sin and corruption. I was never that comfortable with big-time sin and corruption, and now that I'm old and ugly and pooped out—well, I said good-bye to all that some time ago. Now it's just cold meat and rice on the bus after the show.

When I went for a swim this afternoon, there was a young, long-legged girl in a pink bikini getting some sun. Dark, gorgeous, Persian or Israeli, perhaps. Her fingernails and toenails matched the suit exactly, and so did her BlackBerry, on which she seemed to be texting the whole time. A major TV Baby, Satan's daughter.

I sat under the burning Texas sun for a while, reading the *Times*. I finally caught a Mexican waitress's eye.

"Could I order a lemonade, please?"

"Yes, sir. Absolutely!"

JULY 18

Once again, the ambling ghost of Fess Parker intersects our path. In 1955, the elders of San Antonio, Texas, after noticing the influx of tourists following the final episode of the Davy Crockett series—Davy buys the farm when the Mexicans invade the Alamo, which is right here in town—got some Disney architects to look at the river, resulting, many years later, in a sort of San Antonio Land, which is the present-day River Walk. Our hotel is on the River Walk, and that's why I was awakened earlier than I wanted to be by a loud mariachi band just outside the window. I wrenched myself out of bed and stumbled outside, having noticed a pool in a Spanish garden the night before. In daylight, this turned out to be a shallow pit filled with greenish syrup and jammed with children.

Okay, some food. Strolling along the River Walk, I realized I'd left my wallet in my room. I walked back, now in a black mood, hating the tourists, especially the ones wearing T-shirts that say things on them, walking billboards for companies and stores and teams and bands and health clubs and who knows what all. We sell our own at the gigs, for chrissakes. Also hats, cups, mouse pads, all that garbage.

I'm back from the show. The house was a legion of TV Babies, maybe tourists from Arizona. I don't know. Probably rightwingers, too, the victims of an epidemic mental illness that a British study has proven to be the result of having an inordinately large amygdala, a part of the primitive brain that causes them to be fearful way past the point of delusion, which explains why their philosophy, their syntax and their manner of thought don't seem to be reality based. That's why, when you hear a Republican speak, it's like listening to somebody recount a particularly boring dream.

In the sixties, during the war between the generations, I always figured that all we had to do was wait until the old, paranoid, myth-bound, sexually twisted Hobbesian geezers died out. But I was wrong. They just keep coming back, these moldering, bloodless vampires, no matter how many times you hammer in the stake. It's got to be the amygdala thing. Period, end of story.

The crowd sat through our versions of some of the great sixties soul tunes, hating them, waiting only for the amygdala-comforting Doobie Brothers hits that Michael sings, Boz's dance numbers and the Steely Dan singles that remind them of high school or college parties. They despised the old Ray Charles tune, and I started to despise them. Toward the end of the show, during McDonald's piano introduction to "Takin' It to the Streets," I think I really made Carolyn and Catherine uncomfortable by walking back to their riser and telling them, as a way of venting my rage, that I'd been imagining a flash theater fire that would send the entire audience screaming up the aisles, trampling each other to get to the exits, ending up in a horrible scene outside on the sidewalk with people on stretchers, charred and wrinkled. When things aren't going well, the girls, standing just behind me, have to listen to my insane rants. If they're singing, I'll rant to Jim Beard, playing keyboards on the next riser, or, if he's busy, I'll walk across the stage and harass the horn players.

No, I'm not a psycho; it was just a momentary surge of wrath. (Two days later, a bona fide psycho shot up a movie theater in Colorado.) The crowd, they know not what they do. But when I'm fighting exhaustion, putting everything into the performance and still feeling like I'm getting an indifferent response from the house, it's easy to morph into the Hulk. I guess I'm getting more and more thin-skinned as the tour goes on. It's the ATD starting to pull me down, down, down and out.

JULY 19

This morning, the whole band flew to Atlanta to begin the Southern leg of the tour. On the plane, I mentioned to Vince that I regretted my behavior onstage the previous night, bothering the girls with my theater fire scenario. And then Vince revealed this: Not twenty minutes before I was annunciating my terrible vision to the girls onstage, Vince happened to see Pasqual unpacking the laundry backstage so he could put it in my wardrobe case. When Pasqual tossed the weightless plastic wrapping aside, it drifted onto one of the hippie-dippy atmospheric candles in the hall. Vince alerted Pasqual to the ensuing conflagration and he was able to stomp it out. Hmm.

I also found out this: Just like almost every other band, we use a smoke machine to create a haze onstage, which greatly enhances the lighting effects. Every time one of these machines is turned on, theaters have to turn off their fire alarm systems so as not to set them off, which means for the entire length of the show. Think about that, theatergoers.

Anyway, as far as my fiery vision goes, I've never seen any evidence to support the idea of extrasensory perception. What people mistake for ESP, or a case of someone being "psychic"— for instance, someone having foreknowledge of future events or events taking place elsewhere—seems to me to be a matter of intuition based on the conscious and unconscious accumulation of thousands or millions of tiny details. Naturally, some folks are more talented along these lines than others. For instance, my wife is, certainly; I'm not. But I think I might have been pulling in a little ectoplasm last night. No?

JULY 20

A miserable night in the Grand Hyatt. Not a wink of sleep. How can I be the adorable host, the sensitive accompanist, the more or less competent vocalist I'm expected to be under these conditions? I guess it was a mistake to go out last night and see *The Amazing Spider-Man* in 3-D, but after being cooped up on that rotten plane . . .

And then this whole business of changing hotels. When we arrived at the Ritz-Carlton, I realized it was that place I absolutely hate at the intersection of several highways, parking lots and malls in Buckhead. Like, Oh, let's build a luxury hotel in this post–World War III dystopian wasteland. To boot, the lobby and the bar had been taken over by conventioneers from Microsoft, turning it into a scene from *Animal House*, only these TV Babies all reeked of cologne. I panicked. Minutes later, I had Vince check out and we moved down the road to the Grand Hyatt, which was at least a little better—some green things were visible out the windows and so on.

I hadn't seen a film in 3-D since, probably, *Hondo* with John Wayne when I was six or seven. I remember an arrow soaring off the screen and right into my guts. The new 3-D is better, but maybe too exciting for a late show.

Operating on no sleep in my mid-sixties is way different from when I was a kid. I don't run so well on auto anymore. Just now, shaving, I noticed that I'm not thinking practically but, rather, ontologically. In other words, instead of asking myself, "Am I shaving well?" or "Am I shaving cleanly?" I was asking myself, "Am I shaving?" And then, moving on to ethics: "Is shaving the newly grown hair off my face—putting aside, for the moment, the question of whether I leave the sad little goatee alone—a good thing to do? And, even if that is so, is it the right thing to do at this particular time?"

Uh-oh: insomnia tends to come in waves. Maybe I should see if Libby can FedEx me some Ativan.

JULY 21

No need. I bummed an Ambien from Pasqual. I still woke up quite early, but I feel okay. Actually, some therapists recommend staying up all night as a simple cure for simple depression. It's worked for me in the past. In this case, it had the effect of wringing all that boiling, hateful venom out of my body. Last night at Alpharetta, the crowd was my new best friend. Woozy from lack of sleep, I was a combination of Samuel Johnson and Will Rogers, knocking out pithy bons mots, gettin' silly, acknowledging the audience's complicity in life's grand comedy (or so I thought). It had to be a hundred degrees onstage, but the band played like demons. When McDonald went into

"If You Don't Know Me by Now," a middle-aged couple in the first row started making out. On cue, a crack of thunder sounded as we came out for the encore, and as we walked off, a torrent of Georgia rain drenched the happy, cheering crowd.

Storm clouds here too, in Orange Beach, Alabama, on the "Redneck Riviera." It's hot, but mainly it's that the air is heavy with water vapor, like in one of those greenhouses they use to grow orchids. The dressing rooms reek with mold, so I've decided to hang out on the bus. Unfortunately, something has come loose in the ceiling in the back bedroom, resulting in a nasty rattle, especially when the AC is on. At the same time, Vince comes in to tell me that the hotel we had booked for the two days off in Tampa has reported that, due to unforeseen construction, the rooms might be a little noisy. Fuck that. What's more, everything in the area, including the hotel where the band will be staying, is all booked up. Suddenly, the bus is more or less uninhabitable and we have no place to stay starting tonight. But I have another reason to avoid the two-day layover in Tampa Bay. I make plans to get on a flight to New York in the morning.

Late in July 2009, my wife, Libby, was helping Walter shop for kitchen equipment for his daughter. As they walked down Madison Avenue, she turned to him and said, "I know Ezra's dead. I haven't heard from him since July sixth."

Her forty-three-year-old son had moved to Tampa several years before. Looking at his powerful, six-foot-three frame and his strong features, one might not guess that he was a troubled soul who'd had a chaotic childhood and had spent his teen years deep inside the drug culture of the late seventies and early eighties. He'd spoken openly of his suicidal thoughts many times and had come pretty close to pulling it off in recent years. Though his relationship with Libby was tumultuous, Ezra and his mother were so close that it seemed at times as if they shared a single soul. She was tormented by the thought that he might try it again. I had come to love Ez as well and on several occasions had spent long hours on the phone trying to find a way to lift him out of his complex despondency.

Walter tried to make light of Libby's fears. When she got home, though, she tried to contact Ezra by phone and e-mail, without success. On July 30, she checked again to see if she had missed an e-mail. She finally thought to check a rarely used Twitter account and found this from July 9:

From: snarky5000
Ezra to Mom
Had a tooth pulled today—
Now the long, slow, upward march towards death begins—

Libby immediately called his numbers again, with no response. She called the main office of the apartment complex he lived in and was able to speak to the manager, Rhonda, who said she thought someone had heard him "howling at the moon" outside his apartment the night before. But when Libby sent her the Twitter message, Rhonda decided she'd better call the sheriff. At four p.m., Libby called again and asked if the officers had broken into the apartment.

"Yes," said Rhonda.

"Is he alive?"

Rhonda said, "I'm sorry, I can't tell you that."

Libby took a Valium, stared out the window for a while and then lay down on the bed. At six thirty, an Officer Sepulveda called.

"Is this Mrs. Fagen?"

"Yes."

"Are you alone?"

"Yes."

"Your son's dead," said the detective. "Gunshot wound to head."

"How long ago did he . . . ?"

"Well . . . he's covered with bugs."

"No! I want to die too—"

As far as we've been able to find out, Ezra took his own life on his birthday, July 23. Our lives have never been the same, and never will be.

JULY 25

After spending a day with Libby, I flew back to Tampa, played the damn gig in Clearwater and got back on the bus for the ride to Florida's east coast. Libby escaped to Mexico, where she has friends.

No one was waxing the floors or vacuuming when we walked into the lobby of the Seminole Hard Rock Hotel in Hollywood, Florida, at three o'clock in the morning. Like the Hard Rock in Vegas, it's a casino, and it was jumping. Several hundred people were gaming and playing the slots.

The Seminole's main claim to fame is that Anna Nicole

Smith, the blond creature whose tragic life was, thanks to reality TV, also a parody of a tragic life, died in room 607 from an overdose of downers. I remember that the teaser for that mind-boggling, heart-whipping show on the E! network was "We don't know why it's funny—it just is." Wow.

There's a folded piece of cardboard on my night table here in room 1247 displaying a quote from Aerosmith in a script font that reads:

Dream on
Dream on
Dream yourself a dream come true

Not exactly Yeats or Auden, but, as Gore Vidal used to say, shit has its own integrity. I opened up my iTunes and had Paul Desmond, playing live with Brubeck in the late fifties, put me to sleep.

JULY 26

After the Seminole gig, we rode five hours to Jacksonville. I sat up front with Geoff, watching the white line. At four a.m., Vince and I walked into the large, smelly lobby of the Bellevista. After a trek down yet another endless, hallucinatory corridor, we opened the unpainted pine door to an oddly shaped room in which pastel furniture and drapes made of some toxic polymer resin had been installed. Moreover, the room had all the signs that it had recently been the site of a fire, as if someone had tried to dispose of a corpse in the tub with charcoal lighter fluid and a Zippo (there's that motif again). Fleeing the Hotel

Grindhouse, I picked up my bags and headed back to the bus, determined to live the insect life and never get off again.

A lot of the malls and the condos are much nicer now than when I was kid in postwar New Jersey, at the beginning of all that. But, like many of my generation, I'm afraid I'm still severely allergic to all that "plastic," both the literal and the metaphorical. In third world countries, lefties associate it with the corporate world and call its agents "the Plastics." Norman Mailer went so far (he always went so far) as to believe that the widespread displacement of natural materials by plastic was responsible for the increase in violence in America. Wood, metal, glass, wool and cotton, he said, have a sensual quality when touched. Because plastic is so unsatisfying to the senses, people are beginning to go to extremes to feel something, to connect with their bodies. We are all, Mailer thought, prisoners held in sensual isolation to the point of homicidal madness.

Some early Zappa:

Me see a neon
Moon above
I searched for years
I found no love
I'm sure that love will never be
A product of plasticity
A product of plasticity

Now, a half century later, I'm not so sure about that. The Babies seem awfully comfortable with simulation, virtuality and Plasticulture in general. People adapt; they mutate. That's what evolution's all about, isn't it? The concept of love may mutate as well. Some late, oft-quoted Yeats, always bracing:

And what rough beast, its hour come round at last,
Slouches towards Bethlehem to be born?

JULY 27

In the morning, Vince located a pleasant hotel in nearby St. Augustine, the Casa Monica. Unable to find the room service menu, I ate in the hotel dining room.

"How was your breakfast, sir?" the waitress asked.

"Fine," I said. "Except, sitting here in this truly lovely room with the old Spanish woodwork and the big chandeliers with the strings of tiny glass beads hanging down, and with the Florida sunshine streaming in the windows, why does every passing second seem like a thousand years?"

Okay, I didn't say that, but I thought it. And I wasn't even particularly depressed, except for that sort of morning ennui. In the elevator, an old couple, the guy wearing a T-shirt advertising some bait and tackle shop, got off on my floor by mistake and started arguing about which one was the bigger idiot.

At the St. Augustine Amphitheatre in midsummer, you could boil a pot of grits by just setting it on the stage. Plus, it would be impossible to find an acoustic environment less musical than this venue, or more hostile to sonic clarity. All that concrete, aluminum and vinyl serves only to amplify and compound the blowback rather than enhance the music coming off the stage.

Nevertheless, the band, inspired by the wildly responsive, obviously snockered Friday night crowd, laid down the grooves behind the singers and soloists, who were all on fire. For a couple of hours, five thousand people forgot their problems, their grief, the fear of their inevitable appointment with oblivion and were lifted up and out of it by seeing and hearing a hot band play some good music. So there.

The South I get to see is so strange and fascinating. The ancient, white-bearded stoner unloading the trucks, the backstage cooks, the slinky, tattooed and tank-topped Daisy Maes who work in catering. It's so tempting and so awful at the same time, like that old Jimmy Durante song: Did you ever have the feeling that you wanted to go, and still have the feeling that you wanted to stay?

JULY 28

Back to Alabama. The last stop in the South, the Tuscaloosa Amphitheater, couldn't have been more different from St. Augustine.

In the seventies, Walter and I wrote a tune, "Deacon Blues," that toyed with the cliché of the jazz musician as antihero. It was kind of a takeoff on that old essay by Norman Mailer, "The White Negro," not to mention our lives up to that point. I'm sure we thought it was hilarious: the alienated white suburban kid thinks that if he learns how to play bebop, he'll throw off the chains of repression and live the authentic life, unleash the wild steeds of art and passion and so on. The chorus sums it up:

I'll learn to play the saxophone
I'll play just what I feel
Drink scotch whiskey all night long
And die behind the wheel
They got a name for the winners in the world
I want a name when I lose
They call Alabama the Crimson Tide
Call me Deacon Blues

The idea being that this loser is saying, Well, yeah, if mainstream America can buy into this grandiose epithet for a football team, then I want an equally grandiose title. I'm the ultimate outsider, the flip side of the dream, boy-o . . . call me Deacon Blues. (At the time, there was an awesome defensive player on the Rams named Deacon Jones.) The conceit was a bit random, but it sounded good. Though the tune ran really long, it was a hit.

Decades later, when we were back on the road, it had become a thing that when we played in Alabama, especially in Tuscaloosa, where the University of Alabama is, we'd have to play the song. Chances are that none of the people drunkenly screaming for us to play "Deacon Blues" knew or cared what it was about. They just wanted to hear the words Crimson Tide in a popular song.

Anyway, the Dukes never rehearsed the tune. Somewhere along the line, someone had tried to remind me that the Tuscaloosans would be expecting to hear it, but it didn't register. I mean, the song's got, like, a thousand chords. But now, for some reason, I got into a panic thinking that, if we didn't play the song, a phalanx of huge, boozed-up linebackers would charge the stage and string me up from a poplar tree. I walked over to the band's dressing room. Most of the rhythm section said they knew the tune, but we didn't have the horn charts with us, and those guys always need to be looking at music. I had the piano tech, Wayne Williams, find the lyrics, just in case.

My anxiety remained high when the crowd turned out to be the least responsive yet, especially when we played songs other than the Dukes' hits. It was a Saturday night, but they just weren't in the mood. They mostly just sat on their hands and stared, at least until we played the bunched-up hits at the end. I kept hoping that Boz, who's from Texas, or Mike, who's from Missouri, would get them on our side with some of that good ol' Southern-fried humor. But they seemed just as helpless as I was. Had the entire audience gone to the same libido-strangling Fundamentalist school? Had they been body-snatched by aliens? Seriously, it was as if they'd just crawled out of their coffins, brushed the dirt off and sat down. Or were they just so smashed by eight o'clock that they were literally paralyzed?

Maybe we just sucked. In any case, the Deacon Blues thing turned out not to be a problem. There were just a few savage bellows for the tune during the encore, easily ignored. I guess all those younger TV Babies were no longer familiar with the tradition, so we escaped unharmed. At least physically.

JULY 29

Sunday, flying home to NYC. Tomorrow's off, then two shows at Manhattan's Beacon Theatre. Libby home from Mexico tomorrow night. My general condition? In free fall. Smoking? Yessiree.

AUGUST 1

Hometown gigs are a drag. Because of all the guests (friends, relatives, doctors, etc.), there's a climate of agitation that, in my case, I believe, affects the performance itself. Before a show, I try to evoke and maintain a condition of mental clarity and controlled energy, which is to say, I play a lot of R&B records on my computer and drink twelve cups of coffee. The knowledge that all these familiar people will be auditing my every move puts me off balance—it wants to confuse and paralyze, to enervate. It's not about affection for the visitors, or the lack of it, or even self-consciousness, but the difference between feeling free and being superglued to the earth.

AUGUST 4

The two nights at the Beacon were okay. The first night, Irving was there, stopping off on his way to Ireland to play golf with other leprechauns, or something like that. Also Ron Delsener, the big boss man of New York concert promoters. Although I'm pretty sure he's mostly retired from the promotion business, he's still in the business of being cutely crazy. He wears very natty suits. He calls a cab by standing in the middle of the street and yelling, "Mohammed!"

Also there: my cousin Jack and his family, my friends Pete and Neil from high school, and an elite selection of NYC doctors who've kept me and my wife ticking over the years, including a famous brain surgeon. And a lot more people, too.

On the second night, our friend Rick Hertzberg came with his son (and my old pal), Wolf, who's now fourteen. Peter, an old friend of Libby's who owns a bar downtown, told an exciting story: When he was renting some mansion in LA in 1980, an armed robber strolled in the front door while he and his friends were having dinner and told everyone to get down on their knees. The guy was a nasty fucker, pistol-whipping one of the victims and so forth. Peter, figuring the robber was eventually going to kill someone, made a grab for the gun and, after being wounded in the struggle, actually got hold of the thing and shot him dead. Sheesh. Guys who own bars in the city tend to be pretty tough.

AUGUST 5

We made a day trip to Red Bank, New Jersey, to play at—get this—the Count Basie Theatre. Formerly the Carlton (it was renamed in 1984), it's another old vaudeville house. When I mentioned to the audience that the band was stoked to be playing in Count Basie's hometown, there was an actual deafening silence. Apparently, TV Babies aren't big Basie fans.

According to the theater's website, the joint is a favorite with many renowned musical artists:

"Tony Bennett has called it 'My favorite place.' Art Garfunkel said, 'This hall is to a singer what Steinway is to a pianist.' Lyle Lovett said, 'This is one of the nicest-sounding rooms in the whole United States of America.'"

Yeah, the place looks good, but it sounds like shit. As I've mentioned before, the old theaters often look great, but "standing waves" and other factors create acoustic chaos. At the sound check, I was out front with Joe for half an hour just trying to get the drums not to sound like a broken Vitamix blender in a parking garage. There's really no reason to bring all those expensive German microphones to a toilet like this. No decent dressing rooms, either. I had to shave and change on the bus. Again, somehow, we managed to delude the crowd into thinking they heard some worthwhile music. Lucky for us, they're used to hearing crap sound.

Afterwards, Neil, one of the high school friends who was at the Beacon, showed up again. This time, he brought his wife, Hilary, and their daughter and her husband on the bus for a visit. I hadn't seen Hilary in forty-seven years. She was, hands down, the most beautiful girl at South Brunswick High. Of course, we end up looking like what we've been, which, in Hilary's case, was a suburban mom, about to be a grandmom. And yet, she was the same funny, mysterious creature I knew back then. It was great to see her.

A half century ago, she was a heart-stopping, mercurial blond with the kind of verbal acuity and humor that seem to go along with being the victim of a certain sort of fucked-up childhood. Hilary used to juggle friends from several different school factions. Naturally, the actual boyfriends were good-looking jocks, which infuriated me and my beatnik pals to the point of insanity. And yet, she liked to have us around, in a group or one at a time. We were always at her house, draped on the furniture and chatting with her tipsy, somewhat bohemian mom (I was in her mom's social dancing class when I was twelve).

Thing was, I knew Hilary liked me, but I was too insecure and inexperienced to do anything about it. I had a crippling body image problem: at seventeen, I weighed a hundred and twelve and, even at the beach, almost never took off my shirt.

Once, on a really hot day, she called me up and demanded I accompany her to the Jersey shore. She picked me up in her little green Nash convertible and, scarf and blond tresses flying in the breeze, drove us down to Point Pleasant. Lying there on a beach towel, with Hilary's pale teenage body three inches away, I was afraid I might pass out, the victim of some grievous cardiovascular event. We talked for a while, went in the ocean, brushed off the sand, and then she drove me home.

AUGUST 7

Wolf Trap is an opulent shed in Vienna, Virginia, near D.C. Supposedly, colonial farmers dug a lot of baited pits on the land to deal with the heavy wolf population. They're gone now, I think, leaving only the cool name.

In the afternoon, before I got there, some guy came up to Pasqual and handed him an envelope. He said his late mother was a friend of my mother in the forties, and that he'd found a bunch of photos in a trunk that he'd copied and brought along. Sure enough, in these washed-out printer copies, there's my mother hanging out with a gang of friends at the Tamarack Lodge in 1945, which I assume was a Borscht Belt hotel. They're all sitting on the grass in bathing suits. My mom was definitely a babe back then, with the forties hairdo and the dark sunglasses. Only she appears to be hanging out with some sketchy-looking guy with big ears identified as "Bob." I told Pasqual to get the guy, Stan, some tickets, and I saw him after the show. It turns out that Stan's mom, Florence, was the sister of Les Mintz, also a friend of the family and my eye doctor when I was a kid. But who the hell was Bob?

AUGUST 8

A trip to the Sands Steel Stage in Bethlehem, Pennsylvania. I was here last summer with the Dan. The venue is in the shadow of the old steel mill, a gothic castle made of rusted metal with mighty towers and terraces and catwalks and odd little rooms filled with dead machines. It's really something to see. I guess they have plans to use it to attract tourists when the area is further developed. Last year we were climbing inside the thing and taking pictures, which was amazing, because it's a textbook death trap for stupid kids. No access this year, though.

Meanwhile, I keep getting these e-mails from a man named Karim in Irving's office having to do with this solo album of mine that Warner/Reprise is "releasing" (they must think of entertainment product as prisoners or wild beasts or something) in October. All these questions: Do you like what the art department did with the cover? Could you check the copy for the liner notes? We know you won't do regular TV, but will you appear on Stephen Colbert? How about *Fresh Air* on NPR? Which, normally, would be fine, but I'm so wasted at this point, I actually can't grasp much of what's in the e-mails, which, for some reason, are partly in blue type.

Then there's some really eldritch stuff, like: Are you okay with mastering for iTunes? What does that even mean? The album's already mastered, which was already a pain in the ass. And why bother? Everyone listens to music on rotten little computer speakers or those miserable earbud things.

In 1964, long-playing vinyl records sounded great. It was the age of high fidelity, and even your parents were likely to have a good-sounding console or tube components and a nice set of speakers, A&R, KLH, and so on. All the telephones worked, and they sounded good, too. Rarely did anyone ever lose a call, and that was usually on an overseas line. Anyone could work a TV set, even your grandmother. Off, on, volume, change the channel, period. By then, just about everyone had an aerial on the roof, and the signal was strong: ten, twelve simple channels of programming, not all good, but lots of swell black-and-white movies from the thirties and forties, all day and most of the night. No soul-deadening porn or violence. Decent news programs and casual entertainment featuring intelligent, charming celebrities like Steve Allen, Groucho Marx, Jack Paar, Jack Benny, Rod Serling, and Ernie Kovacs.

Yeah, call me old Uncle Fuckwad, I don't care. William Blake's "dark Satanic mills" of the industrial revolution may have enslaved the bodies of Victorian citizens, but information technology is a pure mindfuck. The TV Babies have morphed into the Palm People. For example, those people in the audience who can't experience the performance unless they're sending instant videos to their friends: *Look at me, I must be alive, I can prove it, I'm filming this shit.*

You know what? I refuse to look at you. You're a corpse. And you prove that every day, with everything you do and everything you say. Wake up, ya dope!

Outside of Amsterdam, there's an experimental "care village" for people with Alzheimer's or dementia that offers "reminiscence therapy." There are several different neighborhoods, each one designed, as the *Daily Mail* put it, to take "residents back to their heyday, before dementia eroded any sense of identity, in what some critics have dubbed a *Truman Show* for dementia patients." For instance, wealthy residents are induced to believe that the people on staff are servants. Working-class types believe that the doctors and nurses are part of their extended family. Everything—the architecture of the houses, the appliances, the telephones—are all of a vintage selected to make the residents feel comfortable in their own remembered time. I see myself walking into the fake Dayton Record Store on West Eighth Street in 1963 and thumbing through the albums in the jazz bins, dialing up a fake girlfriend in the fake phone booth in front of the fake Walgreens, trying to scrape the gum off the heel of my black Verde ankle boots. Where will they find a pair of those? On eBay, I guess.

AUGUST 9

Back from a show at the Wang Theatre in Boston. Decent enough crowd.

But after seven weeks out, ATD tends to trump joy. To boot, my right kidney's been bothering me a bit, probably because of some crystal gravel, tiny kidney stones that I sometimes get. Eventually, they flow through into the bladder and then I'm fine, but it's been hurting for a while now and I can't help obsessing about it every second. I started getting paranoid, like I probably have renal carcinoma. After all, I'm sixty-four, I'm smoking again, I take too many painkillers and my blood pressure's high. I've had microscopic amounts of blood in my urine for thirty years. Let's face it, I'm a dead man.

After the show, I was so tired and despondent that I lay down on the filthy leather couch in the dressing room and started whining for my mommy, Elinor, Bob's pal. I wanted her to sit beside me and put a cold compress on my mind, the way she used to put one on my face when I had severe poison ivy. A few minutes later, Carolyn Leonhart came in and asked if she'd heard me correctly, that I was moaning for Elinor: she's heard this routine before. I said, yes, she heard right, but that I'd get over it.

On the way out of the theater, there must have been twenty-five rabid autograph chasers at the stage door, a big thing in Boston for some reason. Most of these guys are autograph dealers. They come prepared with vintage album covers and expensive-looking, textured, framable white paper. They often want a picture, too, for purposes of authentication. Of course, they always masquerade as fans—like, "Great show, Donald"—even though most of them have been standing outside all night. Usually, I'll ignore them or sign some shit or whatever. Tonight, I wanted to melt them all with one of those Raytheon laser cannons and bury them under the sidewalk.

One more word about my mother: She died, horribly, of Alzheimer's. One time, after not seeing her for a while, I visited her in this nursing home in Ohio. As I walked toward her, she stared at me with great interest and then said, "You know, I've always liked you very much." Not long after that, she was gone. How do you like that?

A couple of days later, I started a lyric for this song "Godwhacker," which Walter and I completed and recorded for a Steely Dan CD. It's about an elite squad of assassins whose sole assignment is to find a way into heaven and take out God. If the Deity actually existed, what sane person wouldn't consider this to be justifiable homicide?

AUGUST 10

While I was away at school in the late sixties, my father got laid off from his job in Jersey. He took the family out to Ohio, where he went into the fast-food business with his brother, my weird, funny uncle Dave. My father even consented to attend fast-food school in Indianapolis or somewhere like that. Unfortunately, of all the franchises Dave could have picked, he chose Burger Chef, which was wiped out by McDonald's after a few years.

When I was a kid, Dave once invented an organization for me and my cousin Jack called the MDMD Club. That's "More Daring than the Most Daring." We'd just make up all these stories in which we'd bring off all these dangerous exploits. I guess that's what Dave and my Dad (and Jack's father too, my uncle Al) thought they were doing when, in midlife, they lit out for Ohio to, as one of Dave's hard-boiled idioms would have it, "bilk the goyim."

Not long after the burger tragedy, I was visiting for a holiday weekend. In the evening, Dave gave me a lift from my sister's house over to my parents' nightmarishly bland apartment, which was in a high-rise building on—wait for it—Chagrin Boulevard. On the way, he took me over to see the Beer and Wine Drive-Thru Warehouse, another of the family invest-ments. It was December, and it was freezing when we got out of the car in this little concrete building with a booth where you'd drive up and pay for the crates of wine and/or beer that you load into your trunk yourself. Because it was late, the place was closed. After standing there for a while in a puddle of spilled beer, Dave, wearing one of those hats with earflaps, said, "You know, Donny, sometimes I just want to put a shotgun in my mouth and end all this nonsense."

Which wasn't totally shocking. As I said, Dave was a funny guy. Thing was, Dave's father, who was also my father's father, that is, my grandfather, had gone into his basement thirty years before and done exactly that.

"Yeah, well," I said, "things'll probably start to look up pretty soon."

"Right," said Dave.

Both my mother and father died in Cleveland, in this century. I'll be there on Monday, after weekend gigs in Rochester and Toronto. My sister and her family still live there, but I haven't been in contact with her since my father's death. (It's a long story.) I'm planning on seeing a friend from college who's a doctor at the Cleveland Clinic, though. I'm hoping that Richard can get someone to do a CAT scan of my kidney. It still hurts. I'm also starting to worry about what appears to be a spider bite on my elbow that I got onstage at Wolf Trap. A couple of years ago, in Woodstock, a spider, maybe a brown recluse, bit me on the chest while I was asleep. It itched like crazy for a few days and started to spread. It turned out that the spider had injected a necrotizing toxin, and I had to take antibiotics to stop it from eating off all my flesh. I still have a scar. My elbow's starting to itch a lot now too. I can just see myself in two weeks on the flight home from Indianapolis, a melancholy skeleton sitting there eating airplane food.

AUGUST 11

The Rochester gig turned out to be a solid gas. Joy trumps ATD, for a change. Good crowd, good enough sound, nice vibe all around. In a house where I'm able to hear some detail in the monitors, there's no better job than being in a good rhythm section. If it's jazz, there's more freedom, but juicy groove music has its own thing. Also, as the piano player, not to mention the bandleader, I'm not confined to always playing the same part, though that's fun too. When everything's working right, you become transfixed by the notes and chords and the beautiful spaces in between. In the center of it, with the drums, bass and guitar all around you, the earth falls away and it's just you and your crew creating this forward motion, this undeniable, magical stuff that can move ten thousand people to snap free of life's miseries and get up and dance and scream and feel just fine.

Wait, I'm in too good a mood. Somebody, stop me, please.

AUGUST 12

When we crossed the border into Canada for the Vancouver show a couple of weeks ago, they had us sit in the office (bright fluorescent lighting, uncomfortable chairs) while immigration searched the bus. I got called up to the counter. A guy in a uniform held up a tiny white pill.

"Donald, we found this on the floor in the back bedroom. Is this your property?"

I looked at the pill. "I believe it is."

"Can you tell me what this is? You notice it has a little 'V' inscribed on it."

"Mmm," I said. "I believe that's a Topamax. I take them for migraines."

"And you have a physician's prescription for these?"

"Yes, I do."

"Well, it was lying on the floor back there. Would you like your property back?"

"I guess."

He gave the Topamax back, and that was that. Tonight, crossing over to go to Toronto, a young immigration officer told me to come through a door into a hallway. I assumed it had something to do with the Topamax again.

"Donald," he said, holding up a piece of paper, "are you this same Donald Fagen who has an arrest record in New York State?"

"What? No. I've never been arrested," I said. Then he had me look at the paper. All the birth and family info seemed correct. Then, down at the bottom, there was a flag from the FBI, saying I'd been arrested for selling drugs in 1969.

"Wow. I can't believe I'm seeing this," I said. "When I was in college, they arrested a bunch of students in a raid and I was totally framed for selling pot. The case was dismissed, and, at the time, my lawyer said he had managed to have my arrest expunged from the record, the leverage being that the accuser, a 'sheriff's deputy,' had perjured himself. Have you ever heard of G. Gordon Liddy?"

"No, sir, I haven't."

"Back then, you see, he was running for deputy DA of Dutchess County, New York. He staged the raid on Bard College to get the anti-hippie vote. Then, a couple of years later, Liddy was picked up for being one of the Watergate burglars."

The Canadian copper stared at me for a moment and took the paper back. "Well," he said. "I see you've been in Canada on many occasions. I don't know why it came up this time. It's a really old arrest and I believe you. You should try to have the record corrected, though, because it could keep you out of Canada in the future." And he let it slide.

So, forty-three years later, I now find out that the FBI has a file on me. Vince and I got back on the bus and headed for Toronto.

Pasqual wasn't so lucky. After a hopeful meeting with a dude from Canadian immigration in New York, they still refused to let him into the country, citing old U.S. tax issues and an ancient drug thing. Imagine how many actual psychos they let in just this week: Cyril "The Foot Collector" Gerhardt, Floyd "Rodeo Clown" Van Loon or whoever. O America, O Canada . . .

At the show at the Molson Amphitheatre in Toronto, when the band started the intro to Ray Charles's "Tell the Truth," a TV Baby near the front actually yelled "Fuck you!" and left in a huff with his girlfriend. I guess he only wanted to hear our radio hits from the seventies. You could cut the guy some slack and say that, despite all the PR we did to inform people what the Dukes' Rhythm Revue was all about, he was justified in being put out because he paid for two tickets and his expectations weren't met. On the other hand, you could deduce that he was a rude, ignorant, incurious, racist douchebag that his parents should have been ashamed of conceiving, except that they were probably rude, ignorant, incurious, racist child abusers themselves.

AUGUST 13

Day off. I'd never been to the Cleveland Clinic before. Because of the huge numbers of patients they process every day, they've developed a highly evolved bureaucratic style. A simple visit with a doctor requires a registration with the clinic and then another similar process with the department you need to see. To avoid errors, you are asked the same questions many times over. Through all of this, the staff members maintain an affable but professionally aloof demeanor that started to grate after a while. I could see how a patient could quickly go all cuckoo's nest in this place dealing with the friendly but neutral face of posthumanism. Or maybe it's all hospitals.

My friend Richard arranged for me to see a Dr. Monga, who sent me for a CAT scan. As I suspected, it's just gravel. I'm going to live after all.

AUGUST 14

The show at the Jacobs Pavilion was also fun. Wiggy crowd. Afterwards, Richard and his wife, Margaret, visited the bus. I had invited Dr. Monga, the kidney guy, and he and his wife came too. No use trying to get any interesting scripts from these guys, though—not a writing croaker in the bunch. These days, doctors are terrified that if they prescribe painkillers, or anything that's actually comforting, they'll go to jail like that idiot who shot up Michael Jackson with propofol. Even the familiar "rock docs," local doctors who treat musicians in exchange for permanent backstage privileges, won't prescribe anything useful anymore. I couldn't even get a shot of cortisone for my incredibly itchy spider bite. Oh, well. If all my flesh isn't eaten away by necrotic bacteria, maybe I'll end up with some of that spidey sense, like in the comic books, or I'll be able to make great bounding leaps and crawl up the wall. Put it in the act.

Which reminds me: Last summer, Walter mentioned this guy, the Banana Man, who used to come on the *Ed Sullivan Show*. Occasionally some geezer will bring up Señor Wences or the Old Philosopher or those guys who spun the plates, but I hadn't thought about the Banana Man in fifty years. His whole act was, he'd come out with a big overcoat and keep finding bananas in his pockets or in his pants, strings of them that would get progressively longer and longer. Every time he'd find another string of, like, twenty bananas, he'd pull them out of his clothes while making a surprised sound, like this gurgly *"Whoooooooo!"*

Now that was entertainment.

AUGUST 15

I'm weary of the rock-and-roll tour now and I want to go home. Sleep deprived, Libby deprived, I'm in the bus, finally on my way to perfect Gregor Samsa–like insectitude. The bus is in the parking lot of the Toledo Zoo, where there's a stage. It's drizzly today and the place looks pretty shabby, but, then again, so do I. No real dressing rooms here. The stage is backed by a band shell that's made of a special acoustic metal that turns music into garbage. The only good thing is that, for some reason, the

Leonhart siblings were on the bus this morning and brought Vaughn, Carolyn's four-year-old, who's visiting. He said he liked turkey. I asked him if he ate turkey with the feathers, the feet and the beak still attached and he said yes, he did. Annie, the nanny, said, That sounds disgusting, and Vaughn said, No, it's yummy-disgusting.

Because of the out-of-phase-sounding acoustics due to the band shell and the freaky blowback, the band was not on its game tonight. The audience didn't seem to know the difference, or maybe they did and didn't care.

Tomorrow's off, at the Henry Hotel in Dearborn, Michigan. I've got a long Stravinsky playlist on the Apple and that's what I've been listening to every night to go to sleep: the Odes, *Le Chant du Rossignol, Apollon Musagète, Pulcinella, Symphony of Psalms* and so on. It's really ill to wake up in the middle of *The Rite of Spring*—it's like waking up with the bed on fire. I also now have a small photo of youngish Igor on the desktop of my laptop, one in which he's staring into the camera with that look that's supposed to terrify pitchy violinists.

This latest recurrence of Igormania led me to watch a film streamed from Amazon, *Coco & Igor*, about a supposed affair between Stravinsky and Coco Chanel when Chanel invited the recently exiled Russian and his family to live at her high-style digs outside Paris. The film starts earlier, in 1913, when Coco attends the infamous premiere of *The Rite of Spring* and sits right through the riot, seemingly fascinated by the nutty new music. She doesn't meet him again until seven years later, when she invites him to work at her house. And yet, for the rest of the film, we watch this curiously buff Stravinsky apparently *recomposing* the *Rite* on Coco's piano. This paradox is never explained. I guess the filmmakers couldn't resist the idea that when Igor got to shag Coco, he was inspired to compose this wild, atavistic, new kind of music, in a sort of reversal of George Clinton's slogan "Free your mind and your ass will follow."

In truth, by the early twenties, Igor was actually through with that stuff and had retreated into a more conservative "neoclassical" phase. It's much more likely that Coco, who would eventually become a Nazi spy, fucked Igor into a reactionary spin that would last for the rest of his life. Good music, though.

AUGUST 16

The Henry is a hotel in Dearborn, Michigan, Henry Ford's hometown and the headquarters, I think, of the Ford Motor Company. This morning I actually managed to get up and accompany Catherine, Carolyn, Vaughn and his nanny to the Henry Ford Museum, a huge building filled with old cars, planes and other relics from the history of motored transportation, including a massive Allegheny locomotive, the Lincoln in which Kennedy was murdered, Rosa Parks's bus and the Oscar Mayer Wienermobile. Vaughn had a great time with the trains.

I was going to ask if they had a vintage copy of *The International Jew: The World's Foremost Problem*, the first of Ford's screeds blaming the Jews for all the world's ills, but I chickened out. Igor wasn't that crazy about Jews either, probably because he was often assumed to be one, with that nose and all. There's a story that, on a bus, a grateful fan once addressed him as Mr. Fireberg.

AUGUST 17

After the Detroit show, on the road, late, heading toward Inter-lochen, Michigan, which is a music camp with a theater and a lake. Walt Weiskopf, one of our reed players, spent a summer there. He remembers the theater, but he doesn't remember the lake. How do you like that?

We're about an hour away, and I just saw a sign that said:

PRISON AREA

DO NOT PICK UP HITCHHIKERS

Does that mean that the prisoners frequently escape, roll down the embankment and try to thumb a ride? There's your screenplay right there, folks: Magwitch, the scary escapee (let's give him a Cockney accent; why not?) rolls down the hill, pulls the sign right out of the ground and throws it in the bushes. He's picked up by a crew bus jammed with happy, drunken roadies on their way to Wisconsin. Years later, having made a fortune in the . . . er, um . . . cheese business, he becomes the whole crew's anonymous benefactor. No? Okay, no worries— the Banana Man's got a million of 'em.

AUGUST 18

As I've mentioned, Boz and Mike mostly sleep on their buses, forgoing the hotels. Last night Boz's driver drove straight to the gig, the music camp. He found a place to park near the stage and they all sacked out. Early in the morning, one of the roadies was watching as campers set up chairs and music stands on the lawn facing Boz's bus, a whole symphony orchestra's worth. I guess it was their regular outdoor practice spot. Kids with instruments soon took their places—I'm talking about a huge string section, trumpets, tubas and trombones, woodwinds, a full percussion unit with tympani, giant cymbals, everything. I don't know what piece they were rehearsing, but apparently it was a real flag-waver, double forte. Our man couldn't stop laughing as Boz's bus quickly revved up and moved to a more restful location.

AUGUST 22

After the Milwaukee show we took a day off in Chicago. After sleeping for a thousand years, never leaving the room, I'm now on the bus heading toward a gig in nearby Highland Park for the Ravinia Festival. Three more gigs and I fly home. My spider bite is beginning to heal.

All that sleep and yet I feel strangely unrefreshed, still tired and kind of jumpy, perhaps indicating the beginning of Post Tour Disorder. It's probably going to take several more millennia of sleep before I feel better. It always does.

The show at Ravinia, the summer home of the Chicago Symphony Orchestra, was, I don't know, tight and polite. It's that kind of place. In a desperate attempt to deal with my agitated mood, I asked Pasqual if I could have a tiny toke on one of his thin, neatly rolled joints a half hour before the show. This was a very unusual move on my part. I hadn't smoked any pot for, literally, years. The experience was immediately both familiar and sad. Time stretched out, elongating the spaces between the beats. This gave me more time to think about what I was going to play, and more time to execute. On the other hand, I felt dissociated from the event as it was unfolding. Each song seemed to take forever to wind through the arrangement, and I even lost my place a couple of times. On the upside, I felt a little less wired. But, ultimately, it was a classic bummer.

On the way to Indianapolis, an alarm went off indicating some problem with the bus, forcing Geoff to pull over onto the narrow shoulder. Incredibly, the point at which the system shut down left us without lights, including emergency lights. The traffic couldn't see us until they caught us in their headlights. Each time a huge truck hurtled by, the bus would shake and seem to lift off the ground. For a few minutes, we sat there like idiots on the side of the dark highway, and then scuffled off the dead bus to stand in the weeds while Geoff pointed a blinking flashlight at the oncoming traffic.

Just about the time Geoff figured out how to get the emergency lights working, Vince and I were picked up by the Horn/Nerd Bus. We took off, leaving Geoff to try to deglitch the system. Everyone had conked out except Jay Collins, who was watching a DVD of *The Constant Gardener*. Then he turned in as well.

As I sat there, wide awake, thinking about the bus breakdown, two literary references came to mind. The British sci-fi author J. G. Ballard was fascinated by the way in which technology has dehumanized the world, particularly with highways, parking garages and traffic. In *Concrete Island*, a driver crashes through a barrier and ends up on a traffic island below a network of highways. Unable to crawl up the embankment, he has to live on the island à la Robinson Crusoe, scavenging material from his totaled Jaguar (this was long before cell phones).

The other reference was to the last, lovely lines of *Moby-Dick*. After the white whale sinks the *Pequod*, Ishmael is in the sea, clinging to Queequeg's unused coffin:

> On the second day, a sail drew near, nearer, and picked me up at last. It was the devious-cruising Rachel, that in her retracing search after her missing children, only found another orphan.

How cool is that?

AUGUST 23

I was woken up in the Indianapolis Omni by a band outside somewhere, playing a medley of Eagles tunes. A food festival or something. Then we bused to the Fraze Pavilion in Dayton, Ohio.

When my family moved to Ohio, Dayton was the first place they settled. I asked some of the ladies in catering if they remembered the Burger Chef franchise. Nope.

AUGUST 24

Last show, in Indianapolis, outdoors. Super crowd: old stoners, fortysomethings, college types. Afterwards, there was a band dinner at the Omni. Like all last-night get-togethers, there was apprehension and sadness beneath the surface, people worried about the transition into other gigs, other lives. McDonald was already on the bus back to Nashville, Boz up to Maine somewhere. We'd reconvene in October for the trip to Japan.

AUGUST 25

Vince rode with me to the airport, where he was getting a later flight to LA. After all the vexation and euphoria of the tour, I was feeling strangely placid, or, perhaps, feeling nothing. The greeter person, a young black guy, seemed to think I was a sports agent and asked me how to get into the business, but just then we arrived at security and I didn't have to answer. Byebye, Indiana, I've become airborne.

APPENDIX: ACUTE TOUR DISORDER

Definition

Acute Tour Disorder (ATD) is characterized by a cluster of anxiety and dissociative symptoms that develop in response to traumatic events that occur while a person is employed as a member of a rock concert touring band. Symptoms usually arise sometime during the first month of the tour and continue until its conclusion, at which time the onset of Post Tour Disorder (PTD) almost certainly follows. ATD is related to other disorders brought on as a result of severe vocational stress, such as Combat Stress Reaction (aka shell shock).

Causes and Symptoms

Acute Tour Disorder is caused by exposure to traumatic events that occur during a tour. Curiously, the majority of these events are regarded by the participants as being consistent with occupational norms. These include:

- Confinement in vehicles, hotels, dressing rooms, and so on, with the same group of people over long periods of time
- Daily relocation to a new venue (sports arena, "rock palace," casino theater, "summer shed")
- Nightly performances in front of large, rowdy, often intoxicated crowds as well as exposure to amplified percussion and electric instruments at decibel levels that frequently cause irreversible physical and psychological damage

These are all, in fact, stressors that can produce a broad range of symptoms, including:

Anxiety Symptoms

Mania

Panic attacks

Inability to focus

Paranoia

Anger problems ("stage rage")

Bizarre ideations

Replay of traumatic events (flashbacks)

Physical restlessness

Insomnia

Muscle pain and twitching

Headaches

Diarrhea

Dissociative Symptoms

Depersonalization

Derealization

Emotional numbness

Severe depression

Memory loss

Other Symptoms

Inability to carry out and prioritize tasks

Morbid fixations on minor problems

Physical and mental exhaustion

Sexual dysfunction

In addition, high levels of psychic pain and physical discomfort often lead to secondary problems, such as substance abuse, television trance and compulsive, sometimes deviant, sexual behavior.

Diagnosis

Because the patient suffering from Acute Tour Disorder rarely seeks help until the condition has resolved itself into Post Tour Disorder (i.e., until after the tour is over), the diagnostic history is brief. Opportunities for diagnosis usually present themselves after a severe functional breakdown or when some overt behavioral aberration is brought to the attention of law enforcement and/or medical professionals. After an examination of the patient's history has ruled out diseases that can cause similar symptoms, diagnostic criteria can be set as follows:

- The patient presents six of the above symptoms
- Onset of the symptoms was in the first six weeks of the tour and symptoms show no signs of reduction

Treatment

Treatment for ATD usually includes a combination of antidepressant medications and short-term psychotherapy.

Prognosis

The prognosis for recovery is contingent on the intensity and duration of the tour and the patient's previous level of functioning. Prompt treatment and appropriate social support are major factors in recovery. If the patient's symptoms are severe enough to interfere with normal functioning and last longer than one month, the diagnosis may be changed to PTD. Patients who do not receive treatment for ATD are at increased risk for additional symptoms characteristic of PTD: narcolepsy, major anxiety/depressive disorders and concomitant behavioral aberrations.

Prevention

Of course, the best way to avoid ATD is a real-world transformation such as a change of vocation. With this choice, however, unknown factors come into play, often linked to the withdrawal of the hyperattention that is normally bestowed on the patient by audiences, members of the road crew and industry flacks, that is, a steep and sudden reduction of narcissistic supply. In theory, prompt professional intervention might reduce the likelihood or severity of ATD.

Acknowledgments

Folks who've encouraged me over the years or read through the stuff and let me know if I've said anything really dumb include Peter Battis, John Becker, Walter Becker, Virginia Cannon, Marcelle Clements, Deborah Eisenberg, Brooke Gladstone, Karenna Gore-Schiff, Tony Hendra, Hendrik Hertzberg, Gerry Howard, Fred Kaplan, Dick LaPalm, Rita Meed, Peter Mezan, Susan Lyne, Scott Moyers, Richard Ransohoff, Paul Slovak, Wallace Shawn, John Swansburg, Scott Sutton, Rusty Unger, Dorothy White, Andrew Wylie, Hassan Yalcinkaya and some other guys and gals I'm sure I'm leaving out. Sorry, y'all.